Fr. P. J. Gannon, S.J.

Written in Stone
How the Ten Commandments
Strengthen and Heal our World

SOPHIA INSTITUTE PRESS
Manchester, New Hampshire

Written in Stone comprises six lectures on the Ten Commandments delivered in St. Francis Xavier Church, Dublin, during Lent 1936. It was originally published in 1937 by Burns, Oates, and Washboure, London, under the title *The Old Law and the New Morality.* This 2022 edition by Sophia Institute Press includes minor editorial revisions.

Printed in the United States of America. All rights reserved.

Cover design by LUCAS Art & Design, Jenison, MI.

On the cover: *Moses and the Ten Commandments* (1600–1624),
Museum Catharijneconvent, Utrecht, Netherlands,
image courtesy of Wikimedia Commons.

Scripture references in this book are taken from the Douay-Rheims edition of the Old and New Testaments.

De Licentia Superiorum Ordinis
Laurentius J. Kiernan, S.J., *Praep. Prov. Hib.*
June 30, 1936
Nihil obstat: Reginaldus Phillips, S. Th.D., *Censor Deputatus*
Imprimatur: Joseph Butt, Vic. Gen.
Westmonasterii, October 26, 1936

Sophia Institute Press
Box 5284, Manchester, NH 03108
1-800-888-9344
www.SophiaInstitute.com

Sophia Institute Press is a registered trademark of Sophia Institute.

paperback ISBN 978-1-64413-734-5

ebook ISBN 978-1-64413-735-2

Library of Congress Control Number: 2022935449

First printing

Written in Stone

If thou wilt enter into life, keep the commandments.

—Matthew 19:17

Contents

Preface

The subtitle of this work explains its origin and will, perhaps, go some way toward excusing its many defects. It was not possible in six lectures to a mixed congregation to be either exhaustive or technical. Hence, they cannot constitute a treatise on the Ten Commandments of even the most modest proportions. Indeed, I would not venture to offer them in book form at all if I had not been urged rather insistently by many whose judgment could not but outweigh my own.

They pleaded that the Decalogue needed preaching today as never before and that it could not be too much insisted upon. It had always, of course, been exposed to the inroads of passion and at all times imperfectly obeyed. But never since Christianity emerged from the catacombs had it encountered that widespread, theoretical denial that has become quite fashionable of late in certain circles.

And this denial, this overt challenge, intellectually feeble but very noisy and aggressive, constitutes an undoubted danger to all our institutions. It is part of a campaign of sabotage that is powerful to destroy but impotent to create. In weakening the ancient certainties by which men lived, it is leaving them without any chart of life at all. And that way madness lies, a madness that is extending to other than religious or moral spheres and that is raising deep misgivings for the future in the minds of all who are capable of serious thought.

For it is obvious that without categorical imperatives, behind which lie supreme authority and adequate sanctions, there is no hope of any decent standard of conduct among men. The futility of trying to construct a lay ethic based on any of the parodies of philosophy that have held the field in recent times is first of all, evident in logic and secondly, only too tragically taught by passing events. Humanity has really two courses open to it—to get back to clear thinking and right moral principles, or to continue its perilous drift toward the abyss.

Which it will elect to follow, only time can tell. But the issue is with us in its acutest form. If this little volume should prove even the proverbial widow's mite into the corbona of that venerable sanctuary where once men worshipped and found peace, amid the worst vicissitudes of life, I should feel richly repaid for the labor it entailed.

P. J. Gannon, S.J.

Written in Stone

1

God Is the Supreme Lawgiver

I am the Lord thy God....
Thou shalt not have strange gods before me.

—Exodus 20:2-3

All wars demoralize and leave a trail of spiritual as well as material ruin in their wake. History vouches for the fact, and psychology explains the reasons for it. The Irish nation has passed through the ordeal of (1) the Great War; (2) its own particular war with England, which in the North evoked the sleeping ogre of seventeenth century fanaticism; (3) a civil war, notoriously bitter and socially disintegrating. At present, we enjoy the benefits of an economic war, not without its reactions on conduct.

Under these circumstances, it would have been little short of a miracle if we had not experienced a certain loosening of the bonds that hold men together and keep them submissive to law, whether human or divine. We have the same passions as other races and are subject to the same psychological influences as they. Hence, the wave of revolt against tradition, which was a worldwide phenomenon after the Great War, has not left us unaffected. It could not do so; and the various critics, internal and external, who harp upon the manifestations of disorder and moral decline in our midst without making due allowance for the abnormal circumstances of our times, simply show that they are incapable of fair and balanced judgment.

But there are others who deem it patriotic to insist that there has been no loss at all; that we have weathered the great storm uninjured; that we are as faithful as our fathers and forefathers were to the moral code of Christianity. They admit, of course, that much has changed in our midst; but they think that, on the whole, the changes are for the better and that Ireland runs no risk from the subversive tendencies elsewhere operative.

Doubtless, as usual, the truth lies somewhere between the two extremes. Only a very jaundiced eye will be blind to the steadfastness of the great majority of this people to its old ideals. Only one who knows nothing of the heroic struggles waged by plain and inconspicuous folk to work out their salvation through many tribulations, in a time of great and almost universal distress, will proceed to indict the whole nation. But I think also only one who willfully closes his eyes can ignore certain disturbing facts of recent times or deny that we are faced with an ethical crisis as well as a political and economic one.

For this reason, I have chosen the Ten Commandments as the subject of these lectures. The world is drifting away from them, and the undertow, at least, of this tide of revolt is felt even here. We might conceivably be torn from our moorings and carried far from our anchorage. This is not likely to happen by wide-eyed, conscious choice, nor in an hour; it could only occur through a slow and unperceived process such as has taken place in other lands.

The reverent agnostics of the nineteenth century, who found themselves constrained to reverse the famous gesture of Robespierre and decree the non-existence of God, or at least His unknow-ability, were very sure that in doing so they were not imperiling the moral code hitherto associated with His name. Indeed, they asserted that they were only rescuing morality from a false asso-ciation and placing it upon a nobler basis. Men would practice virtue for its own sake, not for such low motives as fear of Hell or hope of Heaven. Foregoing vain dreams of immortality, they would concentrate upon making this world at least a worthier dwelling place for the evolved primate, who was still progressing and might someday culminate in a being as superior to man as man is to the monkey. Morality came from within and could not be imposed from without. It needed no extra-cosmic lawgiver or post-mortem sanctions. Science, always on their lips identified with empirical science, the knowledge acquired in the laboratory, would teach a finer moral hygiene as it certainly taught a better physical hygiene. Religious taboos, it was generously conceded, may have played quite a beneficent role among primitive peoples. But evolution had carried mankind beyond the need of superstition, and for the future, science would replace religion as the guardian of morality. The doctor would supplant the medicine-man, and the psychoanalyst the priest.

So ran the genial thesis. And it was enforced by contrasting the saintly and dedicated lives led by agnostics, and even atheists, with the cruelty, rapacity, and depravity of the various priesthoods that had warred against the emancipation of the human mind. Further, it met with wide acceptance in a world where commerce flourished, wealth abounded, and inventions of every kind were increasing the possibilities of enjoyment for all.

But the skies were soon overcast, and the prospect darkened. Somehow, man's soul protested against being evolved out of exis-tence, and the promised millennium seemed long coming. Greed, fear, impatience, and frayed nerves produced the Great War. In a moment, the whole dream-world of the agnostics went up in smoke and ashes. The younger generation, bitter and disillusioned, turned upon its teachers. Post-war literature became saturated with pessimism and cosmic despair—a literature of frustration and defeat.

But such a state of mind is not permanently possible. Hope revives after the worst calamities; and out of the chaotic ferment of ideas, two clear streams of tendency are slowly emerging—one to the right, another to the left. The former is leading many of the most serious modern thinkers back to the very threshold of the Catholic faith, or even across it; the latter is conducting the obstinate children of agnosticism farther and farther along the road of negation. They are carrying the principles of Spencer, Huxley, Haeckel, and the rest to their logical conclusion. Assuming still as self-evident that the Christian creed is gone, they are sending the Christian code after it and setting up new codes for the guidance of men.

The most radical expression of this tendency is found in a book published in 1932 by our distinguished fellow-countryman, Mr. G. B. Shaw, who writes: "The Ten Commandments are mere lumber nowadays.... The whole ten are unsuited and inadequate to modern needs." What is to replace them? "Mr. H. G. Wells's *Outline of History* and the host of imitations and supplements that its huge success has called into existence." But we are not confined to Mr. Wells and his disciples: "Within the last two hundred years, a body of history, literature, poetry, science, and art has been created by the same mysterious impulse that inspired the Bible. In all these departments, it leaves the Bible nowhere." From the inspired literature, therefore, that runs from Voltaire to Mr. Wells, Mr. Shaw, Mr. Bertrand Russell, Mr. Aldous Huxley, and Sir Arthur Keith shall our new Decalogue be deduced.

Just how, we are not told. But we are informed about the sanctions of the new morality; for Mr. Shaw sees clearly enough that sanctions, natural or supernatural, are required, and he never shrinks from frank avowals. So he declares roundly: "The knobkerry has to be used as far as the way is clear. Mere agnosticism is not enough.... Whoever hesitates to bring down the knobkerry with might and main is ludicrously unfit to have any part in the government of a modern state." Matthew Arnold, with his "sweetness and light," has been replaced by this wild Irishman swinging not a shillelagh but the foreign knobkerry[1] and willing to play Torquemada to the orthodoxy of unbelief!

In an earlier work, he had written: "I am myself by profession what is called an original thinker, my business being to question and test all the established creeds and codes to see how far they are still valid and how far outworn or superseded, and even to draft new creeds and codes." Where the originality lies in hoeing up again the exhausted garden of Voltaire is not very evident; and less evident still the process by which Mr. Shaw arrives at his almost messianic consciousness of a vocation to be a new Moses to mankind.

But he is not alone in the field. He, too, like Mr. Wells, has acquired fame, wealth, and influence by his writings. Hence, he has his cluster of imitators and satellites glittering around him, and shining with a deceptive brightness in the darkness of the modern world, where any vendor of new evangels who has a skillful pen can impress a generation robbed of all its ancient certainties, and

---

[1] A reference to "The Adventures of the Black Girl in her Search for God," a short story by George Bernard Shaw published in 1932. —Ed.

following blindly after any *ignis fatuus*[2] showing through the night. That is the intellectual tragedy of today. The masses take their ideas even on the gravest issues of life from the popular writers of the moment, and they never pause to inquire into their credentials.

Religion and philosophy are now taught to the multitude through the press, the radio, the cinema, the stage, the novel, and those popularizations of science that no scientist reads and most scientists would repudiate. Some months ago, an English Sunday paper published two articles on religion by (1) a lady writer of sentimental novels and (2) a film star famous for her beauty and screen triumphs. Just what authority they possess for dealing with the profoundest of all problems was not explained. But no matter. One had had some mystic experience at the pyramids by night, and the other had memories of the nightmares she experienced in childhood at the thought of Hell until she learned that God was love! After that, all was well with her and everybody else for ever and ever. An agreeable creed and easy of acceptance, requiring no proofs and, of course, receiving none.

In another similar journal appeared a long article on the tragic life and death of Alma Rattenbury.[3] The writer of it was evidently inspired by the best of motives. He made the fate of this poor sinner a peg on which to hang a really eloquent sermon to his contemporaries and an indictment of "our decadent literature, which wallows in moral turpitude and glorifies it." He pleaded for a return to the law of God. But, and here is the startling paradox, toward the end of his sermon, he wrote: "This tragic woman ennobled

[2] A will-o'-the-wisp. —Ed.

[3] Alma Rattenbury (d. 1935) conspired with her lover to murder her husband, the British architect Francis Rattenbury, in 1935. She was acquitted of all charges but committed suicide shortly after the trial. —Ed.

and purified herself by her awful sacrifice of self-execution after all ennoblement had seemed utterly beyond her reach. In the peak and summit of her fate, she made her peace with the moral world and washed away all her sins in her own blood.... Her expiation is utter and absolute."

Words like these from the pen of a good man, really in earnest in his desire to restore the Christian tradition, leave one bewildered. According to that tradition, Alma Rattenbury's suicide was her worst sin, just as Judas's suicide was regarded as the "irremissible sin," the sin against the Holy Spirit. Yet now we are to regard it as a sacrifice — "washing away all her sins in her own blood"! Could anything reveal more completely the mentality of the modern world than that a well-meaning man can utter what is really blasphemy in the full persuasion that he is pleading for a return to God? Nor would it be difficult to discover equally striking instances of this kind nearer home.

The simple truth is that for four centuries now, the sanity and clarity of the European mind have been slowly but progressively undermined, until no error is too gross or palpable for the consumption of some section of our modern intelligentsia. The proof of this is that atheism, which is the surrender of the intelligence in front of the problem of existence, has come to permeate the thought of millions of men and women everywhere.

Between the triumph of Christianity in the fourth century and its disruption in the sixteenth, the theoretic denial of God's existence was practically unknown. To medieval Europe, the profession of atheism would have qualified a man for an asylum rather than the stake. But the self-styled Reformers first poured the most vitriolic abuse upon the traditional theology and philosophy and then proposed a new conception of God that made Him simply and irredeemably unjust. This naturally opened the way for radical disbelief in His very existence. Giordano Bruno, who was burned at the stake in 1600, may well rank as the first theoretic atheist of any significance in Christian Europe.

But the movement he inaugurated did not die with him. On the contrary, it has moved through many phases of false philosophy, until in our own times it has become the basic dogma of the most subversive social and political revolution ever staged. Nor is it confined to the Soviet republics. All over the world today, we find literature, art, and science permeated to a surprising degree by assumptions that are atheistic, though some of the adherents of these views are unconscious of the conclusions lurking in their premises. Others, more clear-sighted, are conscious of the tendency of their ideas, but far from shrinking from the logic of their system, they even glory in it and find in the dethronement of God the enfranchisement of man.

In point of fact, of course, the dethronement of God leaves man a bewildered and despairing animal in an utterly unintelligible cosmos. It robs him of the basis of his sanity, his self-respect, his hopes. It undermines his spiritual and moral life and leaves him without rudder, chart, or compass on a stormy sea, where treacherous rocks and sunken reefs abound, above which no stars shine, beyond which no port looms. If we remember this, we shall understand the spectacle that saddens our eyes today—the spectacle, namely, of a world beginning to resemble a vast criminal asylum: full of neurotic unrest, full of hatred, greed, ambition, lust, murder, and every unrestrained instinct of the brute.

Fittingly, then, does God, in promulgating the moral law, begin with recalling to His people His own existence. On this all pivots, from this all flows: "I am the Lord, thy God.... Thou shalt not have strange gods before me" (Exod. 20:2-3). This might appear at first sight rather a dogma of faith than a precept of the moral law.

In reality, it is both; for dogma and ethics cannot be separated. But the existence of God is something more than a dogma of faith; it is a truth of reason to which the mind attains easily, almost spontaneously, when disturbing influences, such as pride, prejudice, or passion, do not intervene. Indeed, the knowledge of God by reason is logically prior to the belief in God on account of revelation.

Writers like Sir Arthur Keith seem to imagine that by pouring ridicule on the first two chapters of Genesis, they eliminate God. But this only shows their ignorance of the very problem under discussion. Men must somehow by the processes of reason come to know that God exists before they can elicit an act of faith in the truth of His revelation. Theology lies embedded in and rests on philosophy like a vast cathedral on its submerged foundations. Yet many modern rationalists think that by defacing the statuary over the doors of the edifice, they are dynamiting its foundations. They are really like mischievous schoolboys who play with hand grenades but are not versed enough in the very arts of destruction to be truly formidable. Their influence is strictly limited to kindred spirits and that pitiful mass of public opinion that is impressed by noisy assertion and hypnotized by the crudest propaganda.

As this question is of supreme importance, I hope I shall be pardoned for dwelling on it at some length. Most of you derive your knowledge of God through the Church from revelation. You learned your catechism long ago and in the nature of things had neither the time nor the opportunity of going through the long and complicated process of study and reasoning that would enable you personally to appraise the mass of proof upon which the teaching of the Church is based. You live by faith, and you do well. You act quite similarly in regard to 99 percent of what you accept as certain. You rely upon the statements of scientists, mathematicians, economists, and the rest for what you account true in these departments of knowledge. And if you acted otherwise, you would suffer from mental paralysis. The Church asks no more of you than do the masters of any science. If she claims the charisma of infallibility in a certain very restricted sphere, she proves her right to make this claim by arguments that are valid and conclusive. She repudiates the blind faith of Protestantism as a heresy. She says with St. Paul: "Scio cui credidi et certus sum" — "I know in whom I have trusted and am sure" (see 2 Tim. 1:12).

Hence, the Vatican Council[4] explicitly teaches that "God, the beginning and the end of things, can be known with certitude from creation by the light of reason." In this, she is only echoing the words of the Psalmist: "the fool hath said in his heart, there is no God" (Ps. 13:1); the words of the book of Wisdom: "All men are vain, in whom there is not the knowledge of God" (13:1); and, finally, the words of St. Paul: "The invisible things of him, from the creation of the world, are clearly seen, being understood by the things that are made; his eternal power also, and divinity" (Rom. 1:20). Hence, the mind knows God before heart and mind bow down in adoration or faith raises its glad hosannahs to the God of Israel, the God of Isaac, the God of Jacob, or the inexpressibly tender Father of Mercies whom Jesus manifested to us.

In earlier days, this would have been enough, and for most of you it is even now enough. But as it is fairly evident that dark, underground influences are at work today in our midst, seeking by every kind of innuendo, false assertion, and misrepresentation to undermine your trust not only in us your priests and teachers but also in Him whom we preach, I think it well to make you understand, as far as may be, not only what the Church teaches but

---

[4] The First Vatican Council (1869–1870). —Ed.

why. Hence, I will attempt to arm your own souls with motives that will enable you to cleave to God, though the very heavens above us were rolling up in final doom.

Philosophy offers almost a dozen arguments for the existence of God. They constitute a body of proof so convincing that St. Thomas, the master thinker of our history, felt they simply compelled the assent of the trained mind. They labor under the difficulty of being technical and, at first sight, abstruse. They are couched generally in the language of the schools, and this language is remote from your daily modes of thought. Moreover, the propaganda of the last four centuries has aimed most of all at discrediting the whole science of metaphysics, though even Mr. Shaw is honest enough to admit that "there is no surer symptom of a sordid and fundamentally stupid mind, however powerful it may be in practical activities, than a contempt for metaphysics."

Today, I will take just three of the traditional arguments and endeavor to bring them home to you by certain analogies and comparisons that will, I hope, make you see that the metaphysics of the schools are not meaningless formula nor, in the vulgar jargon of communism, "dope for the ignorant."

1. If you are awakened someday from sleep to find you had been transported in unconsciousness into the carriage of an express train hurrying through an unknown country, and you asked a companion, "Where am I? Where did this train start from, and where is it going?"; if then your comrade said, with a patronizing smile, "Ah, my friend, you are under an illusion; this train started from nowhere and is going nowhere," what would you think? At first, perhaps, that the man was indulging in a silly jest. And if he persisted, you would deem him mad; madder still if he said, "You see, this train has been traveling for so long and is yet to travel for

so long that it needs neither start nor destination; it is eternal, going nowhence and nowhither."

Now, when you and I came to sufficient consciousness in life to be able to ask questions, we found ourselves just like such a traveler. We found that we were wayfarers on a globe spinning on its axis, whirling round the sun, and careering with the sun itself through billions of miles of space. To be told, then, that the process had no beginning and would have no end and could have no meaning, and that in a short space we would be thrown off by the side of the permanent way to rot or be devoured by beasts, and that that was the only answer to our questioning, is just to affront our reason. The plain man sees that this is no answer; that motion supposes a term of rest from which it starts, by some propulsion not its own, and a term of rest toward which it tends; and some adequate reason for start, continuance, and conclusion. Now, the term of rest from which the whole process starts, the term toward which it tends, is God: and in Him must be sought and found the explanation of everything in the whole vast cycle of change.

Here, in a pictorial and graphic form, such as a child can follow, is the very first of the arguments by which St. Thomas proves that God exists. I ask you to judge for yourselves: is this "dope" to make you content with a third-class carriage on the way until you are thrown from the window? As an aside, I might further ask whether, seeing how short is our part of the journey, it matters so very much whether we travel first or third class, provided we arrive at a favorable journey's end—not that I want you to be content with a crowded or unheated compartment if you can mend matters without wrecking the train.

2. The second argument is even more easily apprehended. You behold the sanctuary lamp. It hangs in air, suspended from a chain. Now,

whether you can see to the top or not, you know that somewhere up above there is and must be some fixed point of support strong enough to carry both lamp and chain. Suppose once more that some sapiential friend said to you, "That is a naïve, medieval, unscientific explanation. There is no fixed support. The first link sustains the lamp, the second link the first, the third the second, and so on indefinitely. Hence, there is no need for nail or peg above, and the lamp hangs, like an Indian fakir's rope, without any support at all." What would you say to such a statement? You would strike your forehead and whisper "Poor fellow! Grangegorman!" —and leave it at that.[5]

Look out now on life, and what do we perceive? A vast chain of causation that reaches backward and is lost in the mists of antiquity. This chain needs for its support a fixed something outside itself, other than itself, not caused but capable of being the cause of all causes and effects; and this something we call God. And He must exist and must sustain the whole vast chain, or it would simply collapse. Note, moreover, how puerile, how logically inept, is the effort of modern atheism, which thinks by multiplying the links to lessen the need of the primal support. You see, surely, that every added link increases the need of support and enhances our appreciation of the unlimited Power that swings the mighty cosmos "as a trinket from His wrist."

But, say our brilliant moderns, this tells us nothing of His nature. Let us see. The Cause of causes must contain in Himself all the perfections of all the things that He has made—not as they are in themselves but as they are in the creative first principle. But we have intelligence and will. Therefore, He must have intelligence and will—not, as in us, created, limited, and defective faculties

---

[5] Grangegorman is a suburb of Dublin that was once home to a psychiatric hospital. —Ed.

but uncreated, unlimited, and perfect. When, then, we search our inadequate vocabulary for a word expressive of this fact, we find none better than personality; for intellect and will just differentiate us from the lower creation and make us persons. Therefore, God is a personal Being, though personality in Him surpasses ours as the infinite and self-existing necessarily surpasses all creation. But this does not mean that the word applies to Him less than to us. On the contrary, it is true of Him as of us—only so much more true of Him that our minds fall back, blinded by the splendor of a concept to which we reason beyond the reach of cavil but that we cannot comprehend.

Yet we can understand this much at least: that all the fair and lovely things about us, all the perfections of the human soul, all the rich beauty of the world, the purple splendor of an autumn sunset, the golden glory of a summer dawn, the light of love in children's eyes, the song of lark or linnet, the wind in the trees or the grasses, the solemn music of ocean's tides—all these are somehow in God, only raised to the infinite by virtue of His infinitude.

Since this presents some difficulty for the imagination as distinguished from the pure intellect, let me try once more by analogy to ease for you—I cannot do more—the concept of a perfection existing in God otherwise than it exists in a creature. You see the electric light here. You know it is generated by water passing through the great turbines at Ardnacrusha. Hence, we can say that in a very real sense this light preexisted in the waters of the Shannon, yet surely in a very different way. We can go further and say that this light, which dispels our darkness today, preexisted in the long mental travail of the series of true scientists from Galvani onward who developed the theory and devised the machinery of electricity. All things that have been, are, or shall be, preexisted, as in their primal source, in the omniscient mind and omnipotent will of God. And if we ponder forever so short a time on the marvelous achievement of the human spirit, which can evolve light, warmth, and power from the cold and turbid waters of a swollen river, we shall not falter before the mysteries that meet us on every side when we contemplate the nature or operations of Him who made and rules this universe.

3. And this leads to the third and last argument I shall dwell on— the argument from design, which is, perhaps, the consideration that wells up most spontaneously when we look out upon the universe we behold. Modern rationalists stridently deny its cogency. They refer to it contemptuously as Paley's argument from the clock and sometimes irreverently designate the divinity to which it points as the great watchmaker or clockmaker, as others sneer at St. Paul's potter-God (see Rom. 9:20–21). But the sneer is as stupid as it is irreverent. This argument is as old as Aristotle, who certainly argued to the existence of a ruling and guiding mind.

The reasoning is simple enough for a kindergarten student. There are various obvious instances in us and around us of things obviously fashioned somehow for a purpose. The eye was fashioned to see, and its mechanism is so wonderful that the greatest achievement of human inventiveness fades into insignificance beside it. An ant's nest or a bee's hive is not only a marvelous physical contrivance; it is a society in microcosm fashioned on a wonderful plan.

Now, who or what designed the human eye to see? Who gave social laws to ants and bees? Who drew the pattern of the flowers? Who thought out the indescribably intricate arrangement made for the fructification of plant and flower, to say nothing of beast or man? Nature, say the ready reckoners! But nature is a blind agent.

In all nature known to us, man alone has mind, and man never planned the eye with which he arrives into the world.

Parents do not mold the eye of a child. Either, therefore, that most astounding piece of mechanism was planned by the Divine Mind that laid down from the beginning the whole vast scheme of things, or it was not planned at all, and it was not made to see but sees by some happy accident utterly unexplained and inexplicable. Briefly, therefore, the only choice open to us is to acknowledge God or deny purpose to anything we see in the vast field of earthly phenomena. I leave the choice to you; only I beg you not to let yourselves be mystified by the abstruse and undefined jargon used in the series of books published to popularize the idea that somehow evolution explains everything and eliminates God. Evolution, whether a true or false hypothesis to explain certain phenomena of organic life, leaves entirely intact all the data on which the metaphysician relies for his proofs of the Divine existence and attributes. It has not altered them in the least. Curiously enough, though it would take too much time to explain this here, evolution, if proven, would ease rather than complicate one of the problems of the metaphysician and theologian—namely, the purification of our concept of God, as far as the weakness of the mind permits, from every vestige of anthropomorphism. This is the reason why books of atheistic tendency harp on the contrast between the first chapters of Genesis and the modern textbooks of science.

But the existence of God as a truth of reason has no logical connection with the book of Genesis at all. The difficulty has, at this point of the great debate, no relevancy of any kind. Only the writers of such works are too little versed in the elementary science of logic, too unschooled in philosophic dialectics, to understand precisely where and how their objections, such as they are, should be urged. Genesis might never have been written, and still the arguments I have given you would not be altered by one iota.

Hence, we may conclude that God is still in His heavens, still seated on His throne of majesty, still Creator, Lord, and Master of the cosmos we perceive. The vaster this is known to be, the more ought our appreciation grow of One whose dwelling is the light of setting suns — nay, who was before the daystar shone, who launched the myriad constellations upon their long career through incalculable space, who could launch as many myriads more, if He had so chosen, and could do so with as much ease as He could create a grain of sand. Let science then explore creation as far as it can and tell us all it learns about nature's laws.

The more majestic the reign of law that it reveals to us, the more humbly must we bow in adoration before the Supreme Lawgiver. For out of Bedlam,[6] who can speak of law without a mind and will ordaining it? Nor can we find in some pantheistic chimera the Great Mind ordaining all. For pantheism on examination collapses into atheism. It is an intellectual absurdity comparable with the attempt of a man to lift himself up by his own braces. As Schopenhauer said long ago, and Haeckel repeated after him, "Pantheism is only a polite form of atheism." For poets, in whom the imagination has been developed to the detriment of the analytical and logical faculties of the mind, it becomes a wholly deceptive exit from the dark prison house of materialism, where surely no true *vates* or seer can feel at home. But even Kant has warned us against the danger of the imagination in metaphysics. Pantheism, by scattering God into sparks of divinity that temporally inhabit so many million clods of earth called men or, more unintelligibly still, the whole material cosmos, gives an illusionary exaltation to the creature at

---

[6] Bethlem Royal Hospital, also known as Bedlam, is a psychiatric hospital in London. Its name has become a synonym for madness and chaos. —Ed.

the expense of every attribute of the Creator. It is jugglery, more or less sonorous, and always radically obscure; it is not philosophy at all. Karl Marx was more logical than his teacher, Hegel, and carried the premises of the master to a legitimate conclusion — dialectical materialism, though it is not clear how the adjective attenuates the brutality of the noun.

Appendix

Those who find that metaphysics do not "warm them," as Newman said of himself, may be glad to read the noble "Oda Bog" or "Ode to God" by the Russian poet Gavrila Derzhavin, as translated by Sir John Bowring (1792–1872). Even in translation, it is a great poem, comparable with Francis Thompson's "Hound of Heaven." It is a tragic reflection that the Russian language should now be dedicated to world-propaganda of a philosophy of life that eliminates God and reduces man to the status of an automaton worked by "conditioned reflexes" — whatever that may mean, for conditions and reflexes are alike unexplained and inexplicable. Yet we are asked to treat this as a serious answer to the problems of existence, and we are even told it is the harbinger of the millennium!

ODE TO GOD

O Thou Eternal One! whose presence bright
All space doth occupy, all motion guide;
Unchanged through time's all-devastating flight;
Thou only God! There is no god beside!
Being above all beings! Mighty One!
Whom none can comprehend, and none explore;
Who fill'st existence with Thyself alone;
Embracing all, supporting, ruling o'er,
Being whom we call God, and know no more!

God Is the Supreme Lawgiver

In its sublime research, philosophy
May measure out the ocean deep—may count
The sand or the sun's rays; but God! for Thee
There is no weight nor measure; none can mount
Up to Thy mysteries. Reason's brightest spark,
Though kindled by Thy light, in vain would try
To trace Thy counsels, infinite and dark;
And thought is lost ere thought can soar so high,
Even like past moments in eternity.
Thou from primeval nothingness didst call
First chaos, then existence: Lord! on Thee
Eternity had its foundation; all
Sprung forth from Thee: of light, joy, harmony,
Sole origin: all life, all beauty Thine.
Thy word created all, and doth create;
Thy splendor fills all space with rays divine.
Thou art, and wert, and shalt be! Glorious! Great!
Light-giving, life-sustaining Potentate!
Thy chains the unmeasured universe surround,
Upheld by Thee, by Thee inspired with breath!
Thou the beginning with the end hast bound,
And beautifully mingled life and death!
As sparks mount upwards from the fiery blaze,
So suns are born, so worlds sprung forth from Thee:
And as the spangles in the sunny rays
Shine round the silver snow, the pageantry
Of Heaven's bright army glitters in Thy praise.
A million torches lighted by Thy hand
Wander, unwearied, through the blue abyss:
They own Thy power, accomplish Thy command,
All gay with life, all eloquent with bliss.

What shall we call them? Piles of crystal light,
A glorious company of golden streams,
Lamps of celestial ether burning bright,
Suns lighting systems with their joyous beams?
But Thou to these art as the noon to night.
Yes! as a drop of water in the sea,
All this magnificence in Thee is lost:
What are ten thousand worlds compared to Thee?
And what am I then? Heaven's unnumbered host,
Though multiplied by myriads, and arrayed
In all the glory of sublimest thought,
Is but an atom in the balance, weighed
Against Thy greatness, is a cypher brought
Against infinity! Oh! what am I then? Naught!
Naught! Yet the effluence of Thy light divine,
Pervading worlds, hath reached my bosom too;
Yes! in my spirit doth Thy spirit shine,
As shines the sunbeam in a drop of dew.
Naught! yet I live, and on hope's pinions fly
Eager toward Thy presence; for in Thee
I live, and breathe, and dwell; aspiring high,
Even to the Throne of Thy divinity.
I am, O God! and surely Thou must be!
Thou art! directing, guiding all, Thou art!
Direct my understanding, then, to Thee;
Control my spirit, guide my wandering heart:
Though but an atom 'midst immensity,
Still I am something fashioned by Thy hand!
I hold a middle rank 'twixt Heaven and earth,
On the last verge of mortal being stand,
Close to the realms where angels have their birth,

God Is the Supreme Lawgiver

Just on the boundaries of the spirit-land.
The chain of being is complete in me:
In me is matter's last gradation lost;
And the next step is spirit—Deity!
I can command the lightning, and am dust!
A monarch, and a slave; a worm, a god!
Whence came I here? and how so marvelously
Constructed and conceived! Unknown!—This clod
Lives surely through some higher energy;
For from itself alone it could not be!
Creator, yes! Thy wisdom and Thy word
Created me! Thou Source of life and good!
Thou Spirit of my spirit, and my Lord!
Thy light, Thy love, in their bright plenitude
Filled me with an immortal soul, to spring
Over the abyss of death, and made it wear
The garments of eternal day, and wing
Its heavenly flight beyond this little sphere,
Even to its Source—to Thee—its Author there.

Oh! thoughts ineffable! Oh! visions blest!
Though worthless my conceptions all of Thee,
Yet shall Thy shadowed image fill my breast,
And waft its homage to Thy Deity.
God! thus above my lonely thoughts can soar;
Thus seek Thy presence, Being wise and good!
'Midst Thy vast works admire, obey, adore;
And when the tongue is eloquent no more,
The soul shall speak in tears of gratitude.

2

The Duties of Parents and Children

Honor thy father and thy mother,
that thou mayest be longlived upon the land
which the Lord thy God will give thee.

— Exodus 20:12

The fourth commandment seems at first sight restricted to the relations between children and parents. But a glance at your catechism will show you that its scope is much wider. It embodies the principle of authority and ordains, at least by implication, the duty of obedience on the part of all who are in subordination to those who are in any way armed with legitimate authority. It inculcates the need of discipline if social life, in family, city, state, or world order, is to flourish.

This explains the promise annexed to the precept, which means, no doubt, that the blessing of God will rest upon the dutiful child, but it is still more a warning to the people of Israel that on their observance of the commandment, the stability of their institutions, the strength of their nation, and their power to hold the Promised Land against their enemies depend. I propose to consider first the general and wider aspect of the question.

Written in Stone

The most astonishing feature of the political world today is the downfall of democracy. And the downfall is nearly universal; for even where the forms survive, the spirit has evaporated, and rival systems make their challenge more and more felt. Very ironical, also, is this phenomenon. For the downfall has followed almost overnight on the complete triumph of the democratic principle, which only reached its logical development when adult suffrage for both sexes became the order of the day. This had just happened when, lo! the whole system, which seemed the ultimate term of political evolution, collapsed like a house of cards.

Thus, we must face the plain fact that the system of government that best harmonizes the data of political philosophy has broken down before our eyes in its first contact with reality. It has not survived the first trial test. It has simply failed to function; and it has been replaced over most of the world by systems that are frankly contemptuous of the herd and that invoke blood or class or gold or force or fraud as the very basis of authority.

No more shattering refutation of utopian dreams has ever been given by events. The shock to the mind is paralyzing. Are we to admit that there is no philosophy of politics at all? Must we simply abandon the endeavor to establish a satisfactory basis for social order and admit as the law of life the right of might or superior cunning? Must we concede justification to the exaggerated egotism of dictators and despots and meekly bow our heads beneath their yoke? This is surely a dreadful alternative. Yet no practical politician or statesman has as yet discovered a way out or solved the riddle of the Sphinx. With the fall of the democratic idol, we are left bewildered and disheartened in a very dark impasse.

The divine right of kings was absurd enough and led to many evils. But the divine right of the most brutal, ruthless, and even criminal classes to wade through slaughter, arson, robbery, and wrong to the vacated thrones is, on the face of it, a much more absurd doctrine, and one charged with much more terrible consequences for humanity. Yet such is the operative principle of world politics today. In most nations of the earth, we see the will of the people invoked only to be flouted; for the people, deceived by false promises, waken to find they have a new master more despotic than the old and much more efficient in perpetuating his despotism. How did Lenin differ from Nicholas[7] except in the fact that he was a hundred times more ruthlessly competent? He expressed his disdain of civil liberty with a boldness no tsar ever ventured to display. And every ascendancy everywhere that fights or cheats its way to power now proceeds to dig itself in and impose its every idea upon the body corporate by the muzzling of the press, the silencing of public opinion, and the intensive manipulation of education and party propaganda. Liberty and liberalism, as they were hitherto understood, are almost abrogated concepts.

Can they be restored to currency? Not easily, not in a hurry. Democracy has failed because it was undisciplined and unwise. The undoing of the harm done is going to cost the world dear. And it is by no means certain that when the task is accomplished, our European civilization will have survived.

We assume its indestructibility. What right have we to do so? For centuries now, and with malice prepense, men of great influence but little wisdom have been sapping its foundations, and rulers and peoples alike have looked on complacently. To all who pointed out the dangerous tendency of things, they turned a deaf ear. They are doing so still. Only a few weeks ago, one of the oldest of European nations, whose whole history is interwoven with the

---

[7] Nicholas II (1868–1918) was the last tsar of Russia and was martyred by Lenin's Bolsheviks in 1918. —Ed.

glory and triumph of our culture, apostatized openly and in a general election from that culture. In spite of even recent warning, they voted for more and still more of the revolutionary madness that must simply abolish Spain and set up a congeries of warring tribes and classes in what was once a united land. They voted, in effect, for communism and regionalism. They have thus made one more fatal breach in our European ramparts for the inroads of Tartar barbarism. When such things happen, who can be hopeful? Who can see a single sign of returning serenity in our troubled skies?

But what is the cause of all these upheavals—of this orgy of destruction—this crazy process of burning down our home because the roof needs slates or the foundations need underpinning? The basic and fundamental reason can only be found in the mind and heart of man. Confusion of ideas and indiscipline of will are the root cause of the earthquake tremors shaking our whole political and social system to its downfall.

It is futile to reply that that system was imperfect; of course it was. It suffered from many evils: "Rulers lack wisdom," says the Scripture, "and the people perish"[8] It needed reform. But did it call for complete demolition? Is there not some *via media*[9] between encrusted conservatism and subversive anarchy? Does it baffle the mind of man to find out some method of peaceful evolution? Must headlong vengeance and civil bloodshed mark every readjustment to new environment? When a system has outlived its usefulness, is there no means of preserving the real values it created? Why must its noblest buildings go up in flames—its castles, temples, cities, homes, and cultural achievements be demolished or given over to decay? In the old days, civilization perished at the hands of

[8]   Author's translation of Proverbs 29:18. —Ed.
[9]   "Middle road." —Ed.

nomads from without; ours is perishing at the hands of nomads from within. It is the nomadic mind that is ruining the stately edifice reared through fifteen centuries of human travail; and that nomadic mind has its representatives everywhere.

These intellectual nomads do not necessarily wield torch or bomb—often they lack the necessary courage. But they prepare the way for the crowbar brigade. They break down the moral barriers that hold in check the seething passions of men and women who, condemned to suffer by the laws of the universe—laws that no system can alter or abrogate—are taught that their unhappiness is entirely due to existing institutions and will automatically disappear if these institutions are dynamited. As the suffering is very real, very poignant, very blinding, the masses themselves become the dynamite of the explosion, only to discover, to their amazement, that death, sickness, want, inequality, injustice, and tyranny are, if anything, more in evidence than before. Even then they are told that a little more violence is the remedy, a further movement to the left, a more radical break with the past is all that is needed; and, drunk with hatred, they hold on to the courses that have ruined them. They are like drug addicts, craving forever larger doses of the revolutionary cocaine. It is a pitiable spectacle, calculated to fill one with despair. For reasonableness is the only remedy, and reasonableness is as vain a counsel to maddened mobs as to herds of maddened horses.

It may seem, then, a gross exaggeration to say that the fourth commandment is the cure for a disease so deep seated and widespread. Well, I will avoid even the semblance of exaggeration. But I will venture to assert that the violation of it in the past has played a great part in the breakup of our institutions, and the restoration of it in theory and practice is a prerequisite for social reconstruction or political recovery.

Let us, however, guard against misunderstanding. Liberty is a good thing, a necessary thing, the glorious but perilous privilege conferred on us—and on us alone, apparently, in the visible universe—by the Creator. It must be safeguarded, or else personality is lost in corporate tyranny and character is destroyed. This is one of the gravest results of despotism. The idea that Christianity is the enemy of liberty is a peculiarly perverse falsehood. The reverse is true. Never outside the Christian tradition has true liberty existed. No other philosophy of life has succeeded in formulating the principles upon which it rests. And we see all modern systems based on apostasy from God inexorably driven by the logic of their position to the denial of liberty and the destruction of personality.

But liberty supposes the right use of freedom, and it can be utterly undone by the abuse of freedom or by a wrong conception of it. If that be realized, we shall begin to understand how the apparently triumphant liberalism of the nineteenth century has been vanquished so easily and so utterly. It was divorced in most lands from its true philosophic background; it was confused with utter license; it was betrayed by false leadership; it was reduced to inefficiency and futility by an exaggerated individualism; it was turned into a shibboleth and a war cry without having its meaning clearly defined or its limitations established.

Man is free, and his freedom is sacred. But man is a social animal; and the freedom of each, by a strange paradox, sets up immediate restrictions on the liberty of each. No man is free to do such acts as interfere with the rights of others. Immediately a whole host of delicate problems arise; how to adjust the claims of millions of free units so that they can still be free and yet cooperate in all the manifold activities of social existence—an existence, too, that grows enormously more complex as civilization advances!

In such an organism, two things are absolutely requisite: authority to command on the part of some, willingness to obey on the part of the rest. How authority arises in human societies is a question of extreme difficulty. A volume would be required to treat it even in outline; and here I must suppose only this much — that in any community of human beings, there must exist both rulers and ruled; that rulers are bound to rule justly and in the interests of the ruled, for the interest of the ruled is the very *raison d'être* of authority; that the ruled, on the other hand, are bound to obey in all that relates to public order, tranquility, and the common good. Every individual has the right to criticize his rulers' political wisdom; the right to desire a change of rulers, or even of systems; the right to use fair argument and truthful statement — not lies and calumnies — to persuade others in the same sense. But in the meantime, he must obey. No individual has any justification for making his private opinions the ultimate criterion of truth and wisdom. He may not, out of personal pique or desire of revenge, throw a monkey wrench into the complicated mechanism of government just because he is discontented. This is the nomad mind.

Neither can he arbitrarily proclaim that he, personally, does not recognize a given form of government and is therefore not bound by its laws; nor is he free to plot in secret its abolition by bomb or gun. The very heart of the problem lies here. No one cognizant of history can be unaware of the fact that many regimes are mere usurpations. And these would be enthroned forever if every effort to overthrow them were forbidden. I hold no brief for passive submission to usurpation or tyranny, and I admit that the question of how, when, and where it may be resisted by force or forcibly overthrown is delicate in the extreme. There is no rule of thumb for the application of abstract principles to concrete cases, which, again, are always subtly different and make argument from analogy very dubious and dangerous.

On democratic principles, any government existing in virtue of a majority vote of the ruled is legitimate unless its very constitution outrages divine law or the basic principles of natural morality. Indeed, any established regime functioning with satisfactory results and pacifically accepted enjoys a certain prescriptive right not lightly to be set aside. It is a maxim of ethics that in case of a disputed object, the position of the possessor is the stronger. His claim holds good until the other litigant disproves it. And society cannot be kept forever in uncertainty and unrest by the pretensions of individuals or minority groups. That way chaos lies; and the interests of the ruled, the good of the community itself, postulate submission until it is clear either (1) that the rulers never had, and have not now, a valid charter; or (2) have forfeited their claims by tyranny or hopeless inefficiency; or (3) have lost their support among their people and are no longer recognized. Where this last can be tested at a free election, the cure is obvious and easy. The other two conditions are exposed to all the ambiguities of debate. No universal, abstract principle of discernment can be propounded.

But one thing is evident. In the majority of cases, there are certain obvious facts that establish the right of a given system to its existence and arm it with authority. It is then the betrayal of all order and of the commonweal for the individual or the group to refuse pacific acquiescence. And the various pleas by which such refusal is justified are mere sophistry. The peaceful pursuit of its daily occupations is one of the greatest goods a nation can enjoy, and, indeed, it is primarily for the securing of this benefit that civil government exists. That this should be eternally jeopardized by malcontent groups spells ruin for any land. Because only in the humdrum tasks of the day, only by ploughing, reaping, sowing, building, manufacturing, and marketing can a people grow to greatness or even continue to exist. Violent political experiment is exactly like a serious surgical operation. It is only justifiable when medical treatment has failed and the resources of the physician have been exhausted. Further, it calls for a long and even anxious convalescence if the patient is to survive.

Now, there are millions of men in this Europe of ours who seem to fancy that society can live on one uninterrupted series of surgical operations. There are temperaments fundamentally rebellious—recalcitrant to reason, blind to the lesson of experience, and, apparently, indifferent to the multiplied miseries, moral disorder, and social dislocation inherent in all violent upheavals of any kind. They are the nomadic minds I spoke of. They are the revolutionaries of career. They sow not, neither do they reap. They are incapable of obedience but believe themselves capable of rule. They are callous to the sight of blood, inaccessible to pity, void of any sense of responsibility. Their case is pathological. Reason is wasted upon them. It does not move them in the least that the verdict of intelligence is against them, or the teaching of religion and philosophy. They possess in political affairs something corresponding to the "inner light" of Calvinism.

Neither does it matter that they have no plans for the reconstruction of society, or they have plans so fantastic that they might have been conceived in an asylum. No, the present system is rotten; and the first task, the only immediate one, is to blast it from their path. Then, of course, they will know how to inaugurate the millennium. It never occurs to them to reflect on the fate of their predecessors in similar adventures, who either all failed and perished or who succeeded for a brief moment and then were sent to block or scaffold by their former comrades or by some younger and more "progressive" reformers.

History, with all its impressive teaching, is a closed book to them. How is it possible, for example, that anyone who has pondered the lessons of the French Revolution can lightheartedly set out upon the revolutionary career? Behind the Girondins — idealists, philanthropists, poets, philosophers — stalk the Men of the Mountain, the guillotine in their hands; behind the Men of the Mountain, the Directory with the very same guillotine; behind the Directory, Napoleon with the despot's sword. And almost every great revolution in history has run through the like phases, pointing to some fundamental law determining the rhythm of events.

All this has kept me as yet far from the nursery where the children are at play. Yet there is an inner nexus linking up nursery and open forum, whether this echoes to the sound of buying and selling or to the zip-zip of bullets and the crash of shells. Discipline must be learned early. It is in the nurseries and the schools that the fate of nations is decided. The family is the germ cell of the state: on its healthy or unhealthy condition the commonweal hinges. The rebel in the home evolves naturally into the anarch of the marketplace.

Parents, therefore, have heavy responsibilities to God, the Heavenly Father, to the children themselves, and to the country of which these young people must be architects or the destroyers. Parents as a consequence are bound to devote their best energies to the education of their children. It is in their own interest to do so, as it is their duty. It ought also to be their delight, though a growing number of modern parents do not seem to experience it and shirk their duty, gladly devolving it upon others — nurses, governesses, schoolteachers. Now, these have their part to play. But nobody and nothing can adequately replace parental care and parental affection in the molding of children's characters. Nor need we wonder at the revolt and recalcitrance of children who are conscious that their parents are much more interested in anything else than in them. And children are quick to perceive the light in which they are regarded.

The fourth commandment presupposes parents worthy of honor. But that being presupposed, it is directly addressed to children. And its obligatory nature is too clear to need comment. By natural law as well as by formal divine precept, children owe love, reverence, and obedience to their parents. In early years, this obligation creates little difficulty. Most children fulfill it instinctively, with any proper assistance from the parents themselves. It is when childhood merges into adolescence that tension arises and the situation becomes really critical. The young character must grow and develop even as the body. Courage, self-reliance, all that we call character should be fostered not repressed. No wise parent wants a flabby, jellyfish type of young man or girl to emerge from the years of training. On the contrary, every reasonable father or mother will rejoice in the expansion of the youthful mind and the strengthening of the youthful will.

But the very acme of the crisis is now at hand for parent and child alike. No lapse of years really abrogates the commandment. Time, however, subtly, progressively, and yet profoundly changes its application. Parents must recognize this change as both inevitable and desirable. Their young fledglings must one day develop pinions and ultimately quit the nest; and by that time, they should not only have learned to fly but learned also of the dangers and snares of life's skies. The older folk are sometimes to blame in this respect. They will continue to see in the young man of twenty the curly-haired boy who played round their knees, and in the young damsel of eighteen the angel-eyed cherub of seven. It makes them feel too old if they acknowledge that a new generation is moving on to the arena of life and relegating them gradually to the background.

At this stage, parents who have hitherto acted wisely will have won the love and confidence of such children as have not, in some mysterious way, run awry. They will have become trusted advisers and complete confidants of their offspring, who in turn will recognize the right of their parents to know all about their lives, share all their secrets, and advise in all their plans. The whole garnered wisdom of experience is thus passed on, and family tradition preserved. Without friction, without rivalry, and without tragic break or tragic mistake, the torch is passed from aging and failing hands to eager, younger, fresher ones.

Such is the ideal, and let it not be cynically said that it is not often realized in life; for it has been often realized, and is so still, notwithstanding all the voices to the contrary.

But it is impossible to deny that often also it is not realized. Something goes wrong through faults on one side or the other. Alienation of heart divides the growing boy or girl from the sincerest friends and truest mentors they can ever know. And many voices proclaim loudly that today a very chasm has been dug by some malign influence between youth and age. "The young," we are told, "issue their Proclamation of Independence before they can well spell it and cut the connection with father and mother before they have learned to shave."

Just how much truth there is in all this, it is not easy to decide. In many countries, a very precocious maturity leading to a premature declaration of independence is widespread and notorious. In Russia, a perfectly diabolical campaign is in operation for nearly twenty years to uproot and annihilate our secular tradition in this respect. The result has been a problem known as the problem of the young hooligan, which the moral anarchs at the head of affairs have recently set out to "liquidate" — a word they love — by lowering the age at which the death penalty may be applied by several years!

Poor little waifs! Your rulers educate you into hooligans and as soon as you are in your teens liquidate you by the lethal chamber! Even outside Russia, the state is setting up the immoral claim to come between and before even the parents in the training of its subjects. These are torn from the home in their tenderest years to learn to be good citizens of the totalitarian, divinized state, before they have learned to be simply good children. It is putting the cart before the horse, of course, and is as foolish as it is unethical. It must prove disastrous in the end.

But even where no idiotic and inhuman theories intervene, it is very commonly asserted that the thoughts of youth today are not only long thoughts but wrong thoughts, or, at least, very rebellious thoughts. What is certain is that juvenile delinquency seems definitely on the increase. Instances of perfectly appalling depravity, callousness, and almost bestial brutality come before the courts where the culprits are still minors. (I have heard in our own land of a quite young girl—not insane, unless sheer wickedness be insanity—who rolled a huge stone across the Great Southern Railway line and sat in the heather nearby to see the wreck of the Dublin to Cork express. By accident, someone saw the stone and removed it in time.) Escapades, sometimes simply freakish, sometimes truly criminal, are planned and carried out by mere schoolchildren—the technique being learned from the cinema screen.

And, in general, young boys and girls just out of school are more inclined since the Great War to run amok. This is more marked in the case of young girls—perhaps because earlier up the line, convention, training, and public opinion preserved them more than it does now. It is idle to deny that even here in Ireland our young folk, and particularly our young girls, in large numbers at least, have broken away from old restraints and have learned to despise old maxims of conduct.

But exaggeration serves no good cause. The youth of today, in Ireland at least, can bear comparison quite well with previous generations. Their changed attitude toward their elders has historical explanation and excuse. They inherit our mistakes and have to pay the price for our failures. They enter life at an epoch when prospects are bleak and the problem of existence very difficult. As long as they are at school, the way is clear before them. And it is only just to them to say that until they quit school, they are on the whole docile, well-behaved, and very charming. It is when they leave school that modern conditions try their character a little more severely than is good for fallen human nature.

Primary education ends at fourteen years of age. Thus, the vast majority of young people are faced with the alternative of finding work or passing the most critical years of life in idleness, the foster parent of all evil. How can we wonder, then, that a certain percentage go bad and present us with a crop of larrikin boys and hoyden or harridan girls? The wonder is that the crop is not greater than at present. Parental control over such young folk is extremely difficult. How can father and mother, both perhaps over-taxed with the struggle to find food for themselves and their family, watch over the movements of boys and girls growing up with rapidity, their youthful eyes opening on a world full of dangerous examples, their passions straining at the leash, their energies undirected into wholesome channels? Even those who pass through the secondary schools are launched very early. In these hard times, few parents can afford to keep their children at books indefinitely. The young must soon learn to pay their own way. But immediately that they do so, they develop only too frequently advanced ideas of their own importance and adopt an attitude of pronounced independence. They certainly are less amenable to control.

Further, ever since the Great War, youth has, consciously or unconsciously, come to suffer from a profound feeling of despondency. Postwar literature is full of this sentiment. Disillusion, bewilderment, and a sort of cosmic despair haunt mankind. But youth will not sit still under this. They will have pleasure somehow, anyhow, at any price. Hence, the war was followed by a wave of hectic dissipation. The whole world went dance-mad. It was the age of the tango, the Charleston, the fox-trot, of ragtime and jazz. Men and women, young and old, sought in the false glamour of the cinema, in its tinsel splendor and its tainted melodrama, some escape from care and from the realities of an existence grown tragically depressing. Drink was now too costly, so other anodynes for pain were eagerly availed of.

The best of these, the healthiest and most innocuous, was sport. Hence, sport in all its forms flourished and multiplied its votaries in both sexes and in all classes. This in itself was far from undesirable. Indeed, no better safety-valve could be imagined for the superabundant energies of youth. But it involved an utterly unprecedented freedom of intercourse between young men and women. It led to the wholesale abrogation of the old conventions. It played havoc with inherited ideas of decorum in dress and behavior. It produced a cult of the body that was not equally conducive to the health of the soul. It led to mixed bathing and sunbathing in summer, not always under ideal conditions, mixed hiking, mixed cycle tours, mixed camping out, mixed games of every kind.

Now, it is not my intention to condemn all these certainly serious social changes. It is too early yet to decide what they portend or how long they will endure. But that they are in themselves profound and must necessarily modify life a good deal is evident. Further, that they contain dangers of abuse is hardly less clear. For human nature does not change; its passions and frailties remain unaltered; and it is not easy to see how, when older safeguards are swept away, the inherited standards of morality can be maintained. Certainly, if the young will not tolerate surveillance, they must substitute for it new and very stringent codes of honor and behavior for themselves. The fourth commandment would help enormously in this respect. For in almost all the new amusements, the danger lies not so much in the amusements themselves as in the character of the companions, the attendant circumstances, the moral tone and religious outlook of the whole group. If the young are frank and let their parents know where they go, with whom, and for what purpose; if they return home in time; if they exercise the precautions that age and prudence will suggest, then, indeed, changes that otherwise must involve much spiritual loss may even be conducive to the strengthening of character as well as muscle.

Youth would do well to remember the fate of democracy. Men in general had a fair measure of civil liberty thirty years ago. They did not know how to preserve it. They let it degenerate into license, refused to acknowledge the limitations of personal freedom necessary for the balance and integrity of society in general; they gambled with their acquired inheritance and lost all to despots of one sort or another—all fundamentally alike under labels as diverse as Sovietism and Hitlerism. The young folk of today enjoy freedom from control, which would have seemed sheer anarchy to their grandfathers, and still more to their grandmothers. If they abuse that freedom, they will lose it. "The bright young things" of this "brave new world" may—quite unconsciously of course—be preparing the way for the reintroduction of the purdah and the yashmak,[10] or, at least, for the

---

[10] The purdah is a religious and social practice in some Hindu and Muslim societies in which women are kept separate from men

resurrection of Mrs. Grundy[11] and the restoration of that terrible paternal tyranny that was the hallmark of the Victorian age—or so we are given to believe. Stranger things have happened.

---

either by an enclosed room or by all-enveloping clothes. The yashmak is a veil worn by some Muslim women that covers the whole face except the eyes. —Ed.

[11] Mrs. Grundy is a fictional character known for being overly censorious and prudish. —Ed.

3

The Sacredness of Life

Thou shalt not kill.

—Exodus 20:13

Let us briefly recall some facts of modern history that will be within the knowledge of all. Between the years 1914 and 1918, some eleven million men, the flower of the world's youth, were slain in battle or perished from disease. At least as many more were crippled or invalided for life. The Russian Revolution, a sequel to the war, added two million victims more, while seven million little children, the flotsam and jetsam of war and revolution combined, wandered over the frozen plains, like packs of famishing wolf cubs, until hunger, typhus, and cold blotted them out from the census of the living. Fascist apologists admit about two thousand deaths in their march on Rome and afterwards. The Nazis admit little or nothing. But Sir Philip Gibbs vouches for the fact that in the troubled years following its defeat, Germany was the scene of about three hundred political assassinations. And in that memorable purge of June 30 to July 1, 1934, Hitler and his associates, on their own showing, "executed" some seventy former comrades-in-arms, while rumor gives a total running into several hundreds. These were "Aryans." How many "non-Aryans" have perished in the process of race purgation, Jehovah may remember; Herr Goebbels publishes no lists.

The Spanish Revolution has added its quota of victims, and as yet it has not quite got into its stride. We may reckon on many more.[12] In several European lands, political murder has become an instrument of party politics. The year that witnessed Hitler's purge also saw King Alexander and the French Foreign Minister assassinated in Marseilles, Dr. Dollfuss in Vienna, and a henchman of Stalin's, named Kiroff, in Moscow. To avenge the last, the Tsar of Soviet Russia seized nearly 140 of his associates — it was entirely a family quarrel — and executed one hundred and nineteen.[13] In Turkey, Kemal Pasha has replaced Abdul Hamid — and imitated him.

In China, revolution, civil war, banditry, and foreign invasion have been decimating the unfortunate people since they drove out the Manchus and attained freedom! Japan is determined to rescue them from the perils of freedom — at the cost of many thousands of Chinese lives! The Japanese army, impatient to be at the task, has shot off three ministers of the Mikado and an unknown number of lesser personages.

In the United States, gangsterdom has disputed with constituted authority the government of the world's greatest democracy, and a sporadic war of gang with gang, and gangs with police, has strewn the streets of its great cities with riddled corpses; while in

---

[12] The verification of this prophecy has been swift and indescribably terrible; and, like Banquo's mystic glass, it mirrors a lengthening train of ghosts.

[13] Zinovief, Kamenef, and a dozen more must now be added to the scalp belt of the lonely tyrant cowering in the Kremlin. Yet many seek to multiply Moscows in all the countries of the earth.

Mexico, the gangsters have won out in the duel with civilization, and they murder at their leisure to their heart's content. With sardonic humor, they then send representatives to Geneva, where the blood of "mere Papists," unlike that of Abyssinians, calls for no sanctions of any kind!

In South America, Paraguay and Bolivia have fought themselves to exhaustion over the Gran Chaco, which was once known as Green Hell but is now suspected of concealing oil in its waterless jungles. Several other states in that continent have shed blood freely to decide which group of armed bravos shall have the pillaging of the public treasury.

In Abyssinia—well, you read from day to day of the advances of civilization toward the sources of the Nile and its cost. Perhaps thirty thousand lives have already been sacrificed, and the end is not yet.

Even in our own small land, what horrors we have lived through! After the Great War, in which some 50,000 Irishmen died, there came the very ugly "Black and Tan" campaign, costing about 500 lives on one side or the other; and, concurrently, the still uglier war of pogroms in the North, during which at least 464 men, women, and children perished in Belfast alone. Not content with all this, we staged a civil war, in which the fatalities must have come to about 600. Even since these conflicts ended, we have been startled from time to time by base, besotted deeds of thuggery that only criminal lunacy can cover with a rag of political bunting—acts that make the profession of "patriotism" in the South and "loyalism" in the North stink in the nostrils of all who retain a remnant of moral sense.

In view of this synopsis, and it is no more, of the blood-guiltiness of this generation, it may seem ironical to recall to men's minds that God said on Sinai, "Thou shalt not kill." Yet it is only too evident that unless they hearken to the divine command, they will not only incur the wrath to come but turn earth itself into a very shambles or a plain of bones such as the prophet saw in his vision.

Plato once described man as placed on sentry duty by God. Now, a sentry may not quit his post—still less may he turn spear or lance or gun on his comrades-in-arms. He must hold his post and fulfill his duty to his leader and cause until the trumpet sounds recall.

But God is more than supreme commander of mankind. He is Creator, who has called all of us from nothingness. His dominion, then, is complete, absolute, indisputable; comparable with no dominion of creature over creature; based upon a claim transcending every other claim known to reason. As life giver, He is Lord of life and death. We practice, then, an evident usurpation if, in defiance of Him, we either take our own lives or those of others. "Thou shalt not kill" is thus a precept of natural law as well as of divine revelation.

But this general principle of conduct, like every general principle, needs further precision in its application to the manifold circumstances of human existence, and we must seek such precision from the New Testament and from the Church, to which Christ entrusted the duty of guiding His followers in faith and morals. The moment we face concrete reality, we find how hopeless, as a complete rule of faith, a book must be, however inspired, or an abstract code without an authoritative interpreter.

The fifth commandment forbids suicide, which is the direct taking of one's own life and is never lawful. As we did not give ourselves life, so we may not take it away. On this point, there is no dispute among Catholic moralists. There is never a time or set of circumstances that prevents us from fulfilling our duty toward God and our own soul. And for as long as God sees fit to leave us, here we must remain.

But this does not mean that we cannot incur danger to life, and even grave danger, for adequate reason. Without adequate reason, it is foolhardiness and sinful; with such reason, it is fortitude, which in its higher manifestations we call heroism. But the hero does not seek death; he seeks something quite different, and he permits death if death must come—a totally different moral act from taking one's own life. Nor need we stay to determine the nature of the motive beyond saying that it must be a good one and be in proportion to the hazard incurred.

Again, we may not mutilate ourselves or undergo mutilation voluntarily unless this be necessary for the preservation of life or some vital interest. Here, too, the circumstances call for delicate moral appraisal, and where doubt arises, expert advice should be sought from masters of moral theology.

The motive must be a good one. A soldier who mutilates himself to escape from the duties he has pledged himself to perform sins against the fifth commandment. Many did so in the Great War without consciousness of guilt. But this was an instance of erroneous conscience. The action itself was wrong and indefensible.

Neither can we incur physical mutilation to escape inner temptation, because this danger can be met by other means. When Our Lord said, "If thy right eye scandalize thee, pluck it out" (Matt. 5:29), He was using the language of metaphor, and only mental derangement could take this in the literal sense. Similarly, when He tells us, "There are eunuchs who have made themselves eunuchs for the kingdom of heaven" (Matt. 19:12), He was referring, in figurative language, to the counsel of perfection involved in the vow of chastity.

When it is a question of escaping external danger, the case is more complex. We read of St. Ursula and her nuns, who disfigured their faces to escape outrage from a conquering and licentious soldiery. That they meant well and were subjectively justified is clear. But theologians are divided whether their act was objectively right. It was, assuredly, not of obligation. But it was probably permissible, if the danger was clear and imminent. A woman may jump from a high window, with almost certain death awaiting, to escape from the clutches of a pursuing ravisher. This is not suicide.

Similarly, a man may surrender his lifebelt to another after a shipwreck, though he himself must drown. Men may give first place to women and children in the lifeboats on a like occasion, though they know they must perish. A captain may remain until all his passengers and crew are safe. But when this is secured, he may not go down with his ship out of bravado or to escape censure if his escape is also possible. A dispatch-rider in war may give his life to prevent important information from falling into enemy hands. But here again, he may not take his own life.

The precept against suicide has a negative and positive aspect. It forbids any act that immediately aims at the destruction of one's own life. A man can on no account cut his throat, for example, even though this be done as a means to obtain some most excellent end. The means is wrong, and the end does not justify the means, either in Jesuit theology, as you so often hear, or in any other sound code of ethics. Neither can he take poison with a like intention; though Protestant Germans, such as Professor Paulsen, have lavished praises on Frederick the Great because he always carried a phial of poison with him into battle, prepared to take it if he fell into the hands of his enemies, in order to avoid a demand on their part for a heavy ransom from his impoverished country. This was really an immoral proceeding, though he may not have known it. Again, when Hitler gave his victims the choice of shooting themselves and said it was the honorable thing to do, he was wholly pagan in his conduct; and they were right to refuse.

Again, a man suffering agonizing pain from incurable cancer would hardly sin if he refused to eat and keep a body in existence that had become a source of agony to him. It might and would be noble and more Christian to do so. But I doubt if a moralist would lay on him a strict obligation to do so. He may take morphine to relieve the pain, even if it means shortening life (he may not take a fatal dose to end life). He is hardly bound to foster or husband it when recovery is hopeless and continued existence involves excruciating suffering—at least, it is not evident that he *must* do so.

Let it be noted that this doctrine is not intended to encourage this form of protest, which is often ridiculous, inept, and has now become extremely boring to the public. I personally have little sympathy with it. But I realize that it is not a question of personal taste. It is a question of scientific and unbiassed casuistry.

A weighty objection may be raised from the consequences of the hunger striker. It has a tendency to paralyze the operation of the laws. A convicted criminal may by means of it defeat justice and make imprisonment a farce. Hence, the public good may indirectly make the use of it immoral. There is undoubted substance in this contention. But it may be met.

1. For experience proves that the ordinary criminal lacks either the consciousness of right or the strength of character requisite for carrying it through. He rarely attempts it and hardly ever continues it for long. He knows, moreover, that it will not stir public opinion in his case.

2. The difficulty only arises in connection with political prisoners or enthusiasts for some ideal, true or false. These may be divided into two classes: (a) those who are clearly right and are definitely victims of oppression or injustice, either because their jailers have no legitimate

authority, or they are abusing it, or they have not given their prisoners fair trial. In this hypothesis, no harm at all can come from what is in effect a desperate attempt to right a grave injustice either to a community or to an individual. (b) There remain those who are factious, fanatical, and, in point of fact, wrong in their attitude. They proclaim, for example, that they do not acknowledge an authority that is yet obviously legitimate, or they demand political treatment when they are quite simply commonplace criminals. We have here the most searching of all examples we can consider. If these are allowed to prevail, government would indeed be paralyzed. For any prisoner can pretend not to recognize a government or a court or the justice of his sentence.

Let us see if there is an answer. First of all, the prisoner is morally bound to put aside the obstinacy with which he maintains an anarchical attitude.

But let us suppose that he is incurably obsessed with his false notions and believes himself right. Here, once more, we have an instance of a false conscience that robs his act of its guilt for him. He cannot be held guilty of suicide simply because earlier up the line he has embraced some wholly wrong set of ideas. (Unless, indeed, he has sinfully resisted the light in forming these ideas, in which case he might be held to be responsible *in causa*.) Such a man could, for example, receive the sacraments of the Church if his confessor felt sure of his good faith, though the latter would be bound to point out the error of judgment if he saw any hope of success or if he felt that the common good or the avoidance of scandal demanded it.

What, then, about the government or the prison authorities? Must they yield to a maneuver that they see will produce chaos in the state and prevent the functioning of law? I do not think so. The question turns on their own conviction as to their own position. A legitimate government, sure of its charter, sure of the justice of the prisoner's condemnation and treatment, can afford to despise the challenge to its authority and let the hunger striker die if he persists in his defiance. They must offer him food, and they should leave it within his reach. But they are not called upon to do more. I do not think they are bound to try forcible feeding, as in the case of lunatics (unless the prisoner in question be certified insane). They can simply warn the hunger striker that they will not yield under any circumstances and that, if he dies, his death will be on his own head. A few instances of firmness would soon put an end to the fantastical denial on the part of an individual, or a small group of individuals, of the basic principles of civilized government. The hunger strike need not be a serious menace to any legitimate regime governing justly in the name of the people and in the interests of the community.

Thus, the British Cabinet was free from guilt in letting Terence MacSwiney[14] die — if it was convinced of its right to rule Ireland, not otherwise. But everyone who was convinced of the contrary was entitled to regard it as acting tyrannously and its victim as a hero of liberty. And in all cases in which the hunger striker is in good faith, he might receive the Last Sacraments and Christian burial, even if objectively he was wrong. But it would lie within the competence of the Church to declare that a certain regime is legitimate and that the defiance of it constitutes the sin of rebellion.

---

[14] Terence MacSwiney (1879–1920) was an Irish playwright, author, and politician arrested during the Irish War of Independence in 1920. He died in prison after a seventy-four-day hunger strike. — Ed.

But if a man must respect his own life, still more must he respect that of his neighbor; and the fifth commandment is concerned principally with this. There are enthusiasts who press it to such extremes that even the killing of animals is sinful in their eyes, and they become vegetarians. Well, as long as they confine themselves to making this a counsel of perfection, no harm is done. In general, wanton cruelty to sentient beings is a vile abomination, pointing to a fundamental baseness of character. It is a very sinister trait and rouses both our disgust and our suspicion. Nothing in Christian morality affords the slightest support for such a degrading tendency.

But we must not yield to the sentimentalism that puts the animal world almost on a par with man and accords it rights that are really founded on personality and thus reserved to man. It is surely fantastic to suppose that whereas men have always and everywhere in their history, running through the millennia, regarded the animal world as subordinated to their needs and have made it serve those needs even to the point of constituting an important part of their diet, this was and is immoral. Perhaps we shall all become vegetarians one day or subsist upon synthetic food. But that day is far off, and in the meantime, meat and fish and poultry will be eaten without scruple.

More questionable, at first sight, is the slaughter of animals and birds to cater to feminine vanity or male desire for sport. Yet even here, we have no precept of God forbidding these practices. At least, Christian tradition has never so understood the fifth commandment, which is concerned with human life.

Thus restricted, the fifth commandment might seem to forbid the taking of life under any circumstances. Yet once more, history and commonsense force on us the conclusion that under certain circumstances, the killing of other men or women is justifiable.

Hence, murder must be more strictly defined as the unjust taking of the life of another human being. Need I say that this is a very heinous crime—the crime of Cain, under the anathema of mankind from the beginning; a violation of the most primary and elemental right of man, the right to exist. It is unjust to the victim himself, to his family, to the state, to the Creator. Even in the most primitive societies, it was avenged by exemplary sanctions of various kinds, civil and religious. Society feels itself menaced in its own existence when the sacredness of individual life ceases to be recognized.

I have said that there may be circumstances justifying the taking of human life. Pacificism has sometimes challenged this admission and has pretended that Christianity has been false to its Founder's teaching in permitting any exception to the law. But the most ardent pacifist would forget his principles if attacked by an assassin and able to get his blow in first. And society in most times and places has felt constrained to defend itself by the death penalty against the criminals within its fold who betray its corporate rights or murder a neighbor. With very few exceptions, codes of criminal law assume this as evidently equitable. The Christian casuist says nothing about the advisability or inadvisability of abolishing the death penalty.[15] The spirit of Christianity is always on the side of leniency, unless in circumstances where leniency can only prove an encouragement to crime. Hence, when I say that the state *may* establish the death penalty without being guilty of murder, I am not advocating it, or, indeed, touching the practical question at all. If society can protect itself without this

---

[15] In 2018, the *Catechism of the Catholic Church* declared, "the death penalty is inadmissible because it is an attack on the inviolability and dignity of the person" (2267). —Ed.

drastic sanction, then certainly let it disappear. And in all cases, the state must insist on fair trial and wholly convincing proof.

The question of war, again, raises burning controversy. There is hardly any scourge more dreadful than war, more detrimental to the temporal and eternal interests of mankind. It is certainly one of the major evils of the world, and it is obviously rooted in human depravity. But it is often far from easy to determine who is to blame for it. The complexity of life, the multiplicity of outlook, the variety of training accorded to the children of various races, the competition for markets and a place in the sun, the clash of national ideals and interests—these and a hundred other subtle influences produce discordant views and hereditary prejudices that can grow in intensity until the human Krakatoa erupts.

The opposing forces cannot be both equally in the right, but both can be honestly convinced of the justness of their cause. This should teach us a large sympathy even with open enemies—a sympathy, curiously enough, more prevalent among actual combatants than among civilians outside the zone of strife. It follows that the individual warriors on either side may be entirely free from the guilt of murder, and the mass crime must rest on other shoulders; though here, too, it may be difficult for us to fix responsibility accurately.

On the other hand, there may be cases in which right is very clearly on one side. Naked aggression, pleading nothing but the right of might, is not unknown. In that case, surely the nation assailed can defend its national existence. And even in that case, the ordinary soldiers of the army of aggression may be either quite convinced by the excuses of their leaders or may be under such constraint that they must fight or be slaughtered unresistingly. It would be a stern ethic that would lay this obligation on them, seeing that they are not personally responsible for the injustice of their cause.[16]

But, of course, even in war, those who kill in violation of the rules of warfare are not excused from the guilt of murder. Some of these rules flow from the very nature of things—as, for example, that captives of war should be spared both death and torture; that women, children, and civilian noncombatants should be unmolested in so far as military operations permit it; that reprisals on life or property of innocent parties are unjust. The voice of conscience proclaims these things wrong, and the practice of them must be accounted an abuse.

Further, where conventions are framed by international agreement to safeguard these and other interests of humanity, or where civilized custom has softened the rigors of warfare, those who *first* violate such conventions or customs must be held guilty, and they cannot plead necessity as an excuse. When, however, the wild passions of men are once unchained by war, the conventions of peacetime become, in point of fact and for the most part, just scraps of paper. False propaganda flourishes, and mutual recrimination leads almost inevitably to the conditions of the jungle. *Inter arma silent leges.*[17] The voice of humanity is only too likely to be silenced also. The supreme dictate of reason is to avoid the arbitrament of force and to settle national differences by diplomacy and domestic differences by reasonable politics.

But until the conscience of mankind has put war under the ban and has developed some worldwide machinery of arbitration—a

---

[16] Strictly speaking, they are in this case free only to act on the defensive and repel attempts on their own lives. But in modern warfare, this distinction is often hard to draw. Where it is possible, the principle holds good.

[17] "Laws are silent in the midst of arms."

consummation devotedly to be wished for—it is hardly possible for a casuist to declare bluntly that war is always unjust on both sides. If and when such machinery is devised and impartial courts established, then, certainly, the nation taking the law into its own hands would be guilty of mass murder, just as the aggrieved citizen in an ordered state with courts functioning would be guilty in seeking private vengeance. A new and better order of things would render that simply immoral which had been licit when there was no other means of obtaining redress.

Many other problems could be imagined in connection with the fifth commandment. Dueling, for instance, has been steadily reprobated by the Church and has been gradually almost banished from civilized life. It was as inept as it was unethical. And if there were sometimes plausible pretexts alleged for *accepting* a challenge to save one's career, and without intention of killing the opponent, the Church would not listen to them. For one thing, they were too exposed to the danger of abuse.

We can defend by force our lives and property against unjust aggression, but only in the act of aggression, and even in this case, we may not take life if lesser means suffice. We may act similarly in case of immoral assault. But we may not take life simply to avoid calumny, dishonor, or some spiritual evil, because this is not the way to protect such interests.

Euthanasia, understood as painless putting to death, violates the fifth commandment, whether the sufferer desires it or not.[18]

---

[18] Euthanasia is also used to express the taking away of consciousness in one who is already dying (without hastening death). Even this presents problems to the casuist; but they have no relation to the question we are discussing now. Charity demands at least that the patient be warned he is closing his eyes for the last time and must prepare to meet his God. If he has made all preparations and

So, too, does abortion, which is the direct killing of a living babe in a mother's womb.

Surgical science in recent times is able by two relatively simple operations to sterilize both sexes. And this has given rise to certain very grave problems for the moralist. I can only briefly indicate a few principles of solution.

1. If the operation is performed to remedy diseased conditions, or if sterility ensues from some other legitimate operation, no difficulty arises.

2. If it be part of the vast criminal conspiracy called Neo-Malthusianism, it is to be reprobated entirely.

3. The Nazi state is taking to itself the power of sterilizing all those whose offspring are not likely, in its eyes, to prove useful subjects — particularly criminals, lunatics, imbeciles, and those tainted with syphilis or gonorrhea. And their action finds supporters in many other countries. Further, it is logical enough. For in their theology, the state is God, and the physical fitness of the race is the supreme good of life. But all who repudiate this crass idolatry will approach the problem from another angle. How can the state prove that it has authority from God for such conduct? It was often inflicted in earlier times, but civilization has gradually rejected it — and rightly, one would suppose. It is a great "throwback" to revert to it. Further, the mutilation here proposed is really neither cure nor deterrent for crime, and it is

---

desires the relief, it is hard to see why it could not be rightfully administered. See *Moral and Pastoral Theology* by Henry Davis, S.J. (London: Sheed and Ward, 1935), vol. II, appendix II, no. 15, pp. 167–168.

calculated to increase sexual immorality, not diminish it. Again, the state claims the power to decide what is crime. Thus, the Nazi state may tomorrow pass a law making the profession of Judaism or Christianity a crime and proceed to get rid of all such "criminal" groups by sterilization. The possibilities of abuse in this practice are enormous. It is an immense stride forward toward "the servile state" of which Mr. Belloc[19] has long been forewarning us.

4. The mutilation of the diseased or unfit is still less defensible. Even the best medical opinion is divided on nearly all the medical issues involved. But the ethical issues are independent of their findings. Though the two diseases principally envisaged are incurred generally through sinful acts, this is by no means always the case; and, at any rate, these acts are not as a rule civil crimes. The state cannot punish them as such. Hereditary defects are much less capable of this denomination. On what grounds, then, can the state justify the exorbitant invasion of the rights of personality involved in any such legislation? On none! It has other means of defending society than interference with the basic laws of human life and the natural prerogatives of the individual. In his splendid encyclical *Casti Connubii*, our present Holy Father has condemned these errors.

Finally, we may sum up by saying that we must regard human life as sacred from the first moment of its existence in a mother's womb until the last moment of its earthly pilgrimage. The babe

---

[19] Hilaire Belloc's *Servile State* (1912) argues that capitalism and socialism both lead to a kind of mass slavery. —Ed.

unborn has the same rights as the adult man or woman, and any machinations against its existence are attempts at murder and direct violations of the fifth commandment. When a woman has once conceived, in wedlock or out of it, she has committed herself to the safeguarding of the life within her womb; and, whatever the consequences, she must respect the law of God or incur the guilt of criminal abortion. The consequences may well be grave for her—no one denies that. But they do not excuse murder. They should be weighed in advance and fully envisaged before life comes into being. If they are then considered too grave, it is open to her to decline marriage and to avoid illicit intercourse. When, however, she has become a mother, legitimately or illegitimately, she is held by every law, human and divine, to face the consequences.

I need hardly remind you how often in modern society this obligation is evaded and innocent life sacrificed either before or just after birth. It is becoming a hideously frequent phenomenon, even in our own most Christian land; it springs generally from the contempt of the laws of chastity that is spreading like a vast moral plague all over the world. And nothing could prove more clearly than the prevalence of infanticide how subtly the subversive movements of thought and custom in other countries are invading our hitherto sheltered shores.

Yet we in Ireland have less excuse than those in other lands. We, at least, have a recognized code and an authorized interpreter of it. We can know, if we wish it, how to conduct ourselves in all the tangled relations of life. All that we need is an elementary sense of loyalty and discipline. But it is a painful thing to have to confess that many of our people, when tested, show a strange lack of loyalty and a complete want of discipline. Without exactly denying the Faith, they criticize its teaching when that teaching tends to curb any imperious appetite of theirs. They go over, or half go over, to systems of thought diametrically opposed to the Faith. They seek to combine into their puddingstone philosophy elements that simply refuse to coalesce. If ecclesiastical authority points this out, as it is in duty bound, they set authority at naught, but at the same time, they proclaim that they are just as good Catholics as before. At times, it is hard to believe in their sincerity. In any event, the result is chaotic thinking, which leads logically to conduct utterly out of harmony with Christian morality. For between wrong thinking and wrong conduct, there is a necessary connection. And the wholesale bewilderment of the modern mind conditions the growing anarchy of morals that we behold. Only the integral faith, philosophy, and ethics of the Church can lead the nations out of the morass of mud and blood, of hate and greed and lust, and of the hungry sensualism and panicked despair in which they lie embedded.

Herein, Ireland might easily lead the way, thus holding up to other peoples the example of a nation that knows how to rescue itself from a great debacle brought about by the forgetfulness of God and His laws. This is an ambition worth living for, nobler than political gain or economic advantage, far more salvific than wealth or military might—an achievement of the spirit within the power of the smallest nation in the world, and more fruitful for humanity at large than the building of any empire reaching from pole to pole.

4

The Importance of Chastity

Thou shalt not commit adultery....
Thou shalt not covet thy neighbor's ... wife.

—Exodus 20:14, 17

In the history of the Church's expansion throughout the world, we read again and again how its austere law of sexual morality has chilled the nascent enthusiasm of pagan peoples. The Gospel of Christ makes instant appeal to all that is best in man. Its intrinsic beauty of itself points to a supernatural origin. Its very harmony sounds celestial in all ears attuned to such high melody.

But then, not all ears are so attuned. We know that to appreciate what is best in merely human music, a certain standard of culture is necessary. Jazz addicts and ragtime votaries simply switch off the station from which really great opera or oratorio undulates out upon the ether. Musical taste, like literary judgment, can grow degraded by being fed on garbage. Still more, far more, can the soul become blind to spiritual beauty if it voluntarily walks in darkness and haunts the moral underworld of existence.

The passions of fallen nature constitute the real obstacle to the acceptation of the Gospel. Even intellectual difficulties are so subtly interwoven with moral ones that it is quite impossible to disentangle them. All we can say is that the pure of heart see God — that is, if the heart is wholesome, reason functions freely, reaches God easily, and accepts faith joyously. Conversely, depravity, in all its varied forms, raises a heavy mist that obscures the divine radiance that certainly shines through the veil of creation and ought to be visible to human eyes.

Now, if all our passions have this tendency, the sexual passion, perhaps more than any other, can generate the fog that will obscure the vision beautiful. This is *a priori* intelligible, and *a posteriori* proven by the history of mankind. The carnal man does not savor the things of God. How could he? He is of the flesh — fleshly — and God is a spirit. He loves the works of darkness, and God is light. He scandalizes the little ones of Christ and therefore must stop his ears to those stern words of the Master: "Woe to that man by whom scandal cometh!" (see Matt. 18:7).

Yet the sex instinct itself is natural and therefore sinless. It is willed by the Creator, of whom we read "male and female He created them" and who bade them to "increase and multiply and fill the earth" (Gen. 1:27-28). Even after the Fall, when the perfect equilibrium of original justice had been lost, this instinct, grown dangerous now indeed and needing constant watchfulness, remains sinless — as sinless in itself as hunger or thirst. It is the instrument under providence for the propagation and perpetuation of the race. Also it forms the physical element of what should be the most ardent, the most intimate, and the most enduring human companionship. It tends to unite two lives not merely in carnal embrace but in a union of heart and soul that leads to a fusion and completion of personality that strengthens both, augments the happiness of both, and dispels for both, as far as may be, what has been called the cosmic chill—that sense, namely, of utter loneliness in a universe where man, poor, transient, and mortal, seems lost in illimitable spaces, the plaything of incalculable forces, the victim of a destiny cruel and ironical.

I say all this at the beginning because much modern literature is full of fierce upbraiding of the Church, as if she regarded love and wedlock as a sort of tolerated evil permitted to the weakness of the flesh but somehow degraded and degrading, unworthy of higher natures, arguing a deficiency of finer feeling and nobler aspiration.

What wicked nonsense it all is! What a perverse misunderstanding of the Church's teaching! Certainly, she proclaims that those who for higher motives forego this privilege do well and are, so far forth, on a higher plane of living. She still teaches the entirely sane and balanced doctrine of St. Paul to the Corinthians, which is only an amplification of that of the Divine Master—namely, that the celibate state, embraced for supernatural motives and lived up to externally and internally, is a counsel of perfection, pleasing to God and glorious to man (see 1 Cor. 7).

Nor is she going to retract this teaching. Why should she? Is it not obviously true? As true as that he who sells all he has, distributes it to the poor, and sets out with pilgrim staff to preach the gospel is doing something far lovelier than if he were to settle down to the enjoyment of honestly won comfort in a perfectly honorable career. Why will certain critics perpetually travesty the Church's doctrine in order to attack it? So far from begrudging men and women the great human adventure of love and marriage and parenthood, she seals and sanctifies the union of her children with a sacrament.

What she does teach and must teach is that chastity is a virtue: austere, if you will, but beautiful, in both sexes alike—"for purity is the sum of all loveliness as white is the sum of all colors," to use the words of Francis Thompson. Ribaldry may mock at this virtue and has often done so—formerly in the case of men, now even in the case of women. The licentious frequently make a bravado of their degradation and seek to inflict the stigma of physical defect or of hypocrisy and secret vice on those who strive to keep the whiteness of their soul, the integrity of their hearts.

Yet their words ring hollow and insincere. No reasonable being can question the moral grandeur involved in the lifelong struggle with sensual impulse that is necessary if the fallen children of Adam are to walk this world undefiled. Even ancient paganism was not blind to the beauty of chastity. Euripides in one of his most admired choral odes chants its praises; and in our own times, that quaint old adventurer who gave us *Trader Horn* tells us that in Darkest Africa, the same feeling still prevails. He writes, "It is an instinct universal to worship virginity. Same as they do in the Isoga house.... It sure is a worldwide instinct to worship a maid."

By way of contrast, a well-known female writer recently described it as one of the achievements of feminism that women now enjoyed the same privilege as men of sowing their wild oats without reaping the bitter harvest of shame. As if either sex ever possessed such a privilege! But we shall not stay to reason with those for whom reverence for chastity of body and soul in all men and women, according to their state of life, is matter for derision or denial. They are belying not only Christian ideals but the whole secular tradition of our race.

Certainly, it is not an easy virtue, particularly in youth, when the blood courses riotously in the veins, the imagination fills with sentimental dreams, the stern realities of life are veiled beneath the haze of romance, and as yet all the dark and cruel mysteries of iniquity are unknown. God help the young in this their hour of trial! They little know what weighty issues, temporal and eternal, turn on their conduct during adolescence. Not without reason has the sixth been called "the difficult commandment."

But that is no excuse for calling it impossible or seeking to abrogate it. The Church is not unaware of its difficulty. How could she be? She has had nearly two thousand years' experience of human infirmity, and through the confessional, she has acquired an insight into human nature such as no other institution in the world can claim.

She knows, indeed, that the flesh is weak; but she knows also that the spirit can be strong. She claims to possess supernatural assistance for all her children in all their needs. Surely, by this time, she ought to have learned the efficacy or inefficacy of her means of succor. Yet, Cardinal Newman writes, "It is the boast of the Catholic Church that she can make the young heart chaste."

Assuredly, she has often met with failure in her endeavors to stem the tide of passion; but she has also met with success — far more frequent and more perfect than the modern godless and graceless world can guess. If, then, she persists in preaching chastity as incumbent on all, she must know that it is possible for all, provided that goodwill and the readiness to take the steps necessary for safeguarding this virtue are there.

Of course, if people, young or old, will make no effort, no response to grace; if they will yield in craven soul-surrender to the first solicitations of concupiscence; if they will avoid the sacraments when they need them most; if they will expose themselves to situations that put too severe a strain on nature; if they will adopt the fashions, manners, maxims, and modes of life of a social order going bad at the core and reverting as fast as it can to the sheer paganism from which Christianity rescued Europe; if even her children will halt between two sides and oscillate between the Sermon on the Mount and the ethics of atheism—what can anyone expect but the scandalous spectacle of professing Christians rivalling, or even surpassing, avowed unbelievers in all pernicious practices?

Indeed, when Catholics surrender to the prevailing spirit of license on this issue, they often manifest a quite special perversity of heart. They seem wholly possessed by the unclean spirit, seeking, as it would seem, to silence the reproaches of conscience by outraging all the canons of decency. Only in some such way can be explained the humiliating fact that some of the very worst representatives in modern literature of the crude realism so much in evidence everywhere are apostate children of the Church. In our own country, the three names that occur at once to the student of literature in this context are those of men who have been reared in the Catholic tradition. Non-Catholics, equally divorced from the Christian faith, retain, apparently, at least enough aesthetic taste not to degrade the Muses into dirty-minded, foul-mouthed drabs of the street.

For we must admit that these poor ladies, tolerably respectable in their ancient home of Hellas, at least while it still remained great, have in recent times been thus dishonored by many of their pretended votaries. That this is art, or truth, or beauty, or in any way worthy of admiration, or indeed capable of reasonable defense, is entirely false. A well-known Irish writer once described one of his novels as "the best aphrodisiac in literature." What a conception this displays of the function of literature, which has for its formal object truth under the aspect of beauty and is thus bound by its essential purpose to confine itself to the beautiful in life! Yet can anyone seriously maintain that modern realism, with its pessimism, its cynicism, its grossness, has any relation at all to beauty? There is only one adequate description of it, and that is that it is literature in the last stages of degeneracy.

Christians who wish to remain faithful to the traditions of the Church must, therefore, bear in mind that there exists a vast conspiracy of modern intellectuals to destroy the very principles of sexual morality. What they hope to gain by this we can only surmise; their motives may be left to the study of alienists. But their works must be eschewed under penalty of gradual, insidious perversion. Above all, they must be kept away from the eyes of youth. Let us not be overawed by the indignation of these writers themselves or their servile claqueurs in the yellow press.

Immoral literature is spiritual poison, as dangerous as morphine or cocaine. No one proposes that these drugs, which can yet serve most noble purposes, shall be exposed for sale to every purchaser in any chemist's shop. You know, on the contrary, that stringent laws guard the bodily health of mankind. Yet modern liberalism makes the welkin ring at the very mention of safeguards or restrictions where spiritual health is at stake. But then, modern liberalism is largely atheistic — just simply that — in its philosophy of life, and it secretly disbelieves in any spirit — in man or above him. It is the very same false liberalism that has produced the economic and political chaos that we behold around us. If we want to preserve liberty, we have got to scrutinize the pretensions of this liberalism just as closely as we scrutinize the pretensions of Hitlerism or Sovietism. For extremes meet, and the older liberalism was quite as tyrannical, though in subtler ways, as the systems that have arisen out of reaction from it.

Under it, the anti-Christian campaign inaugurated by Voltaire was able to make a conquest of the world and, in its triumph, to turn education, science, history, literature, art, politics, economics, the press, the cinema screen, the theater, and the music hall into so many media for corrupting the hearts of countless millions, and thus weaning them from any faith in anything except the animal in man.

But the Church, though fully aware of the forces leagued against her that are working for the spiritual ruin of her children, and aware also of the weakness of nature, the strength of passion, and the thousands of difficulties created by our civilization for the practice of chastity, still flings her moral challenge in the face of a scornful generation and says, "Thou shalt not commit adultery; thou shalt not covet thy neighbor's wife." Nor is she moved in the least by the apologies for sin with which the whole mental atmosphere is permeated. She rejects as sheer and detestable blasphemy the suggestion, insinuated in so many erotic poems and novels, that because God is love, all love is somehow divine. God is certainly love, and love is the noblest emotion of the heart of man. But there is no word in any language more "soiled with all ignoble use" than that simple monosyllable.

I think, indeed, that we should protest against the employment of the same word to express the sentiment that makes a man a saint, a hero, a sage, a scholar, or a philanthropist and the base, hungry, selfish craving that makes a man a libertine. I can hardly imagine any two things more diametrically opposed. For love seeks the good of the object beloved, even at the expense of self, but lust—the true name for the other sentiment—seeks transient personal gratification at the expense of the object it desires. The former is "strong as death," in the words of Song of Solomon (8:6). The latter is fickle and changeable as the caprices of madness. It is ravenous, exorbitant, and utterly egoistic. At best, it is merely carnal; at worst, it is positively devilish. Over-indulged, it lays waste all the nobler instincts of manhood, all the specific beauty and charm of womanhood. It should be sharply distinguished from love.

But the devil's advocates in this matter are not silenced. They sneer at the very idea of love between man and woman unassociated with physical desire. They style it the mawkish conception of idealists, mostly celibates, who they say know little or nothing of life. They call the sublimation of love the sublimation of absurdity, the attempt to turn a physiological urge—for many of them, a physiological necessity—into a bloodless, bodiless abstraction. If they are Freudians, they go further, and, through a materialistic psychoanalysis, they reduce the very purest and holiest affections of humanity to manifestations of sex. The very ardors of the saints for God and things divine, which are the supreme triumph of spirit over matter, become in their vile pages an allotropic form of carnal passion. It is not only the height of blasphemy, it is the limit of absurdity; and the lengths to which it can be carried by sex-obsessed degeneracy will be understood by those who are conversant with modern literature. No others will have any idea of the studied wickedness of the great campaign against our faith and our ideals that is being waged with an almost incredible malevolence. Never, not even in the declining days of Greco-Roman civilization, was the mental climate more impregnated with the microbes of spiritual plague.

Nor is there any single Christian virtue so virulently assailed as the virtue of chastity. There is no social institution exposed to more deadly attack than the home, which rests on this virtue and must disintegrate without it. In defending it, the Church is literally fighting *pro aris et focis*, for altar and hearth. Neither religion nor domestic life can long survive its overthrow. The student of history knows this as well as the theologian.

It is sometimes said that the Catholic pulpit insists on the sixth and ninth commandments too exclusively, as if they constituted the whole law, and that thus it tacitly connives at the neglect of other important virtues. If this be asserted of any individual preacher, it should be proven, and, even then, nothing would follow but his own one-sidedness. If it be asserted of the official teaching of the

Church, it is grotesquely false. For that teaching expressly tells us that he who offends against one commandment offends against all; which, again, must be rightly understood. The real malice of every violation of God's law is just the fact that it is a revolt against the Divine Will and the divine governance of the world. And thus, the formal element of every sin is found in any sin. Theft is not murder, and murder is not adultery or perjury. But each and all of these involve the same essential malice of rebellion against God.

Further, the Church knows and teaches that the malice of sin lessens in proportion to the antecedent temptation, and she is fully aware of the strength of sexual concupiscence. Hence, she regards the sins of the flesh, the sins of frailty, as much less symptomatic of wickedness of will than the hard and bitter sins such as hate, pride, greed, and cruelty.

But, once more, the Church has two thousand years' experience of human weakness and human misery. Hence, she knows the key positions in her spiritual citadel; she knows where most easily a hostile inroad may be made; she realizes that for every one who may be tempted to murder, ninety-nine will be tempted by sensual appetite. Also, she has learned long ago that, whereas the spiritual ruin of her children begins only too often in weakness of the flesh, it rarely stops there. She has seen in every generation what wholesale devastation unbridled lust can bring about in the moral nature of man; how swift and terrible is the descent of the unchaste; how profound and horrible the depths to which they sink. The libertine must become a liar, a deceiver, a hypocrite; a thief poaching upon the preserves of others; a moral murderer, slaying the souls of others. Nay, how often he ends in physical murder is attested daily in the press we read.

For this reason, the Church does preach chastity insistently, though not exclusively. It is a key position, and she feels that if it is lost, many other positions must fall. She will never cease to proclaim its reasonableness, its beauty, its universal obligation. Further, her teaching is clear-cut and peremptory—more so, perhaps, than all even of her children quite understand. Let me elucidate it:

1. The sex-instinct is implanted in the race for the purpose of procreation. Procreation is thus the explanation and justification of sexual desire or indulgence. This, at a stroke, and by immediate induction, renders hideous and immoral all deliberate venereal pleasure not subordinated to this end. I need not dwell upon the various perverse practices that are thus placed outside the pale of decent or reasonable behavior. St. Paul says of them: "Let them not be even mentioned among you" (see Eph. 5:3). Theoretic defense of them is, indeed, not unknown in these our days; but then, is there anything base enough to be unknown in these days of ours? The defense of them is an even greater abnormality than the practice of them.

2. Yet even the normal appetite calls for strict regulating principles. Mankind has always felt this instinctively. Certain pseudo-scientists in the last century taught pontifically that animal promiscuity was the natural state of affairs in primitive society—a stage through which man had to pass by slow degrees in his evolution from his ape progenitor. But no serious student of anthropology or sociology now defends this thesis. Research has rendered it not only untenable but even ridiculous. For the primitives are known to have often stood, both in religion and morals, considerably higher than their more highly civilized descendants. Marriage

is a well-nigh universal phenomenon of all human life revealed to us by history.

3. Polygamy, frequently, and polyandry, in rare instances, have certainly prevailed here and there. Yet monogamy has been far and away more widespread than those aberrations. The teaching of Genesis is enforced by philosophy and confirmed by ethnology and anthropology. Conscience, that universal monitor, endorses it emphatically. Marriage is a natural institution; and, even as such, it is a lifelong union between one man and one woman for the propagation and education of children. It is indissoluble in virtue of its purpose and character.

4. It is at this point that dissent of any serious kind arises. At all times, the indissolubility of marriage has created difficulties for fallen nature. Mere passion is a flame that burns out in a short time. Love itself can change and even, in sad instances, turn into aversion and repulsion on one side or the other. When this happens, we certainly meet tragedy of a poignant kind. A union that ought to sweeten life may render it bitter as the waters of Mara[20] and become a yoke almost too heavy to bear. And the modern apostate world is loud that it should not be borne—that it should be broken, and the parties freed to seek happiness again in some more propitious experiment.

---

[20] See Exod. 15:23: "And they came into Mara, and they could not drink the waters of Mara, because they were bitter: whereupon he gave a name also agreeable to the place, calling it Mara, that is, bitterness."—Ed.

It is a mistake not to recognize the speciousness of this contention. We gain nothing by not facing it fairly. If the happiness of the contracting parties were the chief end of marriage, the contention would have some weight. But that is just what religion and philosophy must deny. Now, only in lifelong, monogamous marriage can the complete welfare of the child be adequately secured. Hence, the institution, as such, must be lifelong monogamy; and the laws governing it must be based upon this principle. Divorce, therefore, is excluded, just as infidelity is excluded.

Nor is it enough to reply that the interests of the child may sometimes be sufficiently protected even if divorce be sanctioned or infidelity connived at. This may occasionally be true of his bodily and worldly interests—rarely, if ever, of his spiritual interests. But these instances are exceptional. If they are made the determining factor in legislation, the door is opened to all sorts of abuses. The permission of divorce inevitably leads to the multiplication of divorces, until you arrive at the state of affairs that prevailed in Old Rome and is fast coming to prevail in many lands today; while indifference to the fidelity or infidelity of one's partner in marriage is directly opposed to one of the most primal instincts of mankind. The marriage code of Russia today is not only unchristian—it is simply, and in the strictest sense, inhuman. Already we hear that a reaction against it is setting in. Women, in particular, are experiencing the full horror of the attempt to strip love of all romance, all decency, all reserve, and all fidelity. The girl anarchs of 1918—and there were plenty of them—are beginning to find that they are now deserted by their casual lovers and have no children's love to console them—for their children belong to the Moloch state—no Heaven to hope for, no shrine to pray at—nothing, in fact, but burnt-out ashes in a cold grate.

Even if the marriage be childless, it is none the less indissoluble. For, once more, the institution derives its unalterable laws from its general purpose and cannot be imperiled by concessions to circumstances or the inconsistency of human hearts. If childlessness were an excuse for divorce, what injustice would often be done to women! They would be cast out and penalized quite frequently for a failure due, as often as not, to the partner, not themselves. Further, anyone can see how such a condition of things would lead to the most crying abuses in modern times, when criminal devices for the frustration of nature's purpose put it in the power of either party to keep the door always open for a change of partners by having no children until he or she wearies of the consort. The teaching of the Church may seem in certain instances severe and unbending. But that is only because the Church envisages the totality of life and watches over the human hearth with little less solicitude than it guards the altar of God.

Further, though its solicitude embraces both sexes and their rights impartially, still, in point of fact, the Church's legislation stands like a strong rampart around the weak things of life, the woman and the child. Is it not monstrous, then, that some of the most bitter assailants of its teaching today are women? I know, of course, that they are not very numerous—but, oh! they can be so noisy, so ignorant, and so shameless. I have seen the statement in feminist propaganda that St. Paul is responsible for the deplorable condition of inferiority and slavery in which the sex has hitherto existed. They do not tell us who was responsible for its still more deplorable condition of servitude and humiliation in every land, epoch, state, or culture outside the Christian tradition. Logic is certainly not their strong point, and argument is wasted on them. I would only warn Christian women to beware of their utterly unhistorical and foolish diatribes. Christianity, and it alone, has enfranchised the sex; and it did that nearly two thousand years before they got a vote, which it never denied them but never agitated for, perhaps because it knew that the vote means, in the ultimate analysis, just a scrap of paper. In trying to teach both men and women chastity, it did more for women than all the codes of law ever tabulated or ever to be tabulated until time is no more. And if in this most difficult undertaking it has had but indifferent success, women hardly less than men have been responsible for the failure of its endeavors.

God help us all that we should be forever chasing the mirage and vainly dreaming that we can alter nature itself and reform everybody and everything except ourselves! If only an increasing number of men and women would look into their own souls and try to make their own lives conform to the moral law, what a different place this earth itself would become! If we would really listen to those words of Jesus, "Seek ye therefore first the kingdom of God, and His justice, and all these things shall be added unto you" (Matt. 6:33), we would attain to the kingdom of this world by concomitance. But by inverting the order, we suffer an ironical yet very just punishment; we lose both worlds and flounder forever in the Slough of Despond.[21]

The Church's law of chastity is high and holy; it is austere. I do not deny it. But it is the only law that has ever lifted life above the tyranny of the senses and the bondage of the lusts of the flesh. It is, perhaps, more austere than many quite understand. Let me expound it as clearly as I can: Outside the married state, all deliberate seeking of sexual pleasure, by thought, word, or deed, alone or in company, consummated or unconsummated, is mortal sin; and within the married state, all that implies either infidelity to one's partner or perversion or frustration of the purpose of matrimony is equally sinful.

---

[21] A fictional bog in John Bunyan's *The Pilgrim's Progress* in which the protagonist sinks under the weight and guilt of his sins. — Ed.

Let it be noted that both full deliberation and consent are necessary for mortal sin. But if these are present, then there is no parvity of matter admitted by Catholic theology. Lest this should cause scruple, I make haste to add that the same theology stresses the distinction between sin, which lies in the consent of the will, and temptation, which goes before and wrestles, as it were, to obtain that consent.

Temptation is not a sin, not even a venial sin in itself. And it might be vehement and long-continued and involve no guilt at all.

It is evident, however, that just because of human weakness and blindness, just because of the sometimes-imperceptible merging of temptation into sin, just on account of the confusion that can thus arise, all men and women need guidance and advice. Here, we Catholics have in the confessional not only a sacrament giving us the specific graces needed for our daily fight against the world, the flesh, and the devil but a spiritual clinic wherein we may obtain skilled advice — nay more, wholly authoritative advice. On this advice we may safely rely, knowing that in obeying it, we are acting in accordance with the plan of salvation instituted by Christ, who in making the priest a spiritual physician guarantees us from blame even if he should be unintelligent or incompetent, provided that we fulfill our part. The penitent may safely follow such advice and is thus always in a position to avoid the snares of Satan.

But there is the tragedy! Just when men and women need all the aids at their disposal, they are prone to deprive themselves of them, and, sometimes out of perversity, sometimes out of a false humility, they delay going to Confession in time. Then, when they fall, they keep away still longer through false shame or spiritual sloth or gradual hardening of the heart, until they lose touch with the sources of grace and the means of salvation. Chastity is not beyond the attainment of any man or woman who lives the

Christian life as it should be lived; but it is not any easier for a professing Christian who does not live up to his profession than for a pagan who makes no profession at all. Perhaps, indeed, it is a little harder; for the worm of conscience always gnawing at the heart produces all sorts of unwholesome internal complexes leading to ever wilder derangement of will. It is a pearl of great price, and the price is ceaseless watchfulness over the imagination, the intellect, and the heart. But no one should ever lose courage, for if the struggle is difficult, the reward is transcendent, even in this life—the succor at hand divine and therefore all-powerful. "I can do all things," says St. Paul, "in him who strengtheneth me" (see Phil. 4:13). It is the tocsin of the Church.

5

On Temporal Prosperity

Thou shalt not steal....
Thou shalt not covet thy neighbor's house ...
nor his servant, nor his handmaid, nor his ox,
nor his ass, nor any thing that is his.

—Exodus 20:15, 17

Every one of the commandments is vital not only for the salvation of the individual but also for the wellbeing of society. None of them can be ignored or widely violated without disastrous results to the whole community. But these results are more immediate and more evident in the case of some commandments than in that of others. The two we consider now are so intimately bound up with the economic and social life of man that they simply govern business intercourse and effectively determine the measure of prosperity any nation shall be permitted to enjoy. They prescribe for all of us the practice of justice in our dealings with our fellowmen; and justice is the very keystone of the arch that bridges over the gulf separating ordered civilized existence from the conditions of prehistory. *Justitia stant magna imperia*[22] was a medieval proverb. Its application is wider: the whole social life of men rests upon the virtue of justice as a pyramid rests on its base. It is literally impossible to exaggerate its importance in the building up of any social structure whatsoever. I need not apologize, therefore, for dwelling upon the definition and analysis of the concept.

Justice is often used in Scripture as the equivalent of righteousness or of the whole duty of man. Here we are envisaging the word in a somewhat narrower or more technical sense. We may define it as the moral virtue that impels us to give to all our fellow men whatever may be their due. Yet more strictly understood, it ordains respect for the rights of property that men possess. Now, that men possess certain such rights I here purpose to assume. That nobody has any strict right to any form of property is too silly a pretension for debate. The limitations of those rights may, indeed, raise all manner of perplexing problems; the existence of them is too deeply rooted in the nature of man, too clearly exemplified in his whole secular history for any reasonable denial.

Neither can I dwell on the various ways in which those rights arise. They are not conferred upon the individual by the state. How could they be? The individual is logically prior to the state. Man is an individual before he is a citizen. The state, rightly conceived, is nothing other than so many individuals organically united into a society that, as a moral entity, has for its sole function the securing of the fullest and most complete life in common of the units composing it. Perhaps one may say that half our modern political blundering is due to a forgetfulness of this fact. The state has been set up as something existing, as it were, in the air: distinct from, prior to, and dominating over the various individuals. It is divinized — literally

---

[22] "Great empires rest on justice."

deified—and set up on the emptied altar of God. This would be bad enough if it were merely an abstract theory with no influence on conduct. So far, however, from being that, it translates itself into practice immediately, even necessarily, by turning the state into a Moloch on whose cruel altar nearly every right of human personality is immolated. If we cannot see this exemplified in the various totalitarian states of today, we can see nothing.

But I may not here pursue this subject further. I assume that man has the right to possess something, and that that right is implemented in a whole host of ways, by any number of contingent facts and circumstances, which result in determining, with sufficient accuracy, the right of the individual A to a given object B. This right must be respected by everyone other than A, including the state itself, though the state may have the power and even the obligation of seeing that A's claim is not exercised to the detriment of the rights of others.

Justice is subdivided by moralists into legal, distributive, and commutative. Legal justice binds a man to respect the rights of the community for the common good. It obliges rulers to just legislation and the ruled to due obedience.

Distributive justice lays upon rulers the obligation of dividing public benefits and public burdens impartially and equitably, in proper proportions, among the ruled. It is the virtue of those in authority.

Commutative justice urges the private individual to render to other such individuals all that is strictly due to them, and in terms of arithmetical equality. It is in this sense that the word is most commonly used; and it is this virtue that is particularly prescribed by the seventh and tenth commandments. We must not steal the goods of another; we must not even covet them deliberately. And under the word "steal" is included every fraudulent transaction.

In recent times, much has been spoken and written about what is called social justice. It raises, however, issues too vast to be even summarily dealt with here. Suffice it to say that it presupposes commutative justice and can neither violate it nor substitute for it. Its basic principles are laid down in the encyclicals of Leo XIII and Pius XI as nowhere else, and the problem of our time is to reduce these to practice. A very admirable discussion of the whole question, by Rev. E. J. Coyne, S.J., marked the Lent of last year and will be fresh in the memory of all who interest themselves in the matter. I am not treating of it at all. I am speaking of commutative justice.

And of this virtue, I say unhesitatingly that it is fundamental for the social and economic life of mankind and imperatively necessary in our dealings with one another. The whole vast machinery of commerce and exchange, of credit and international trade, from simple barter up to the most elaborate operations on the bourses of the world, depend upon it. And every single violation of it is a grain of dust thrown into that complex machinery, tending to clog it, paralyze its operation, and produce economic chaos. Roguery, in all its protean forms, in all its dimensions, whether it be petty larceny or the gigantic swindling of a Krueger, a Hatry, or a Stavisky,[23] makes for the impoverishment of the whole community. It is a crime against society. And if it spreads sufficiently, it can simply ruin a whole social order.

Yet it is undoubtedly today perilously prevalent in all ranks and classes, in all economic relations, in every land. It is an incalculably vast factor in that great crisis that is producing such a

---

[23] Ivar Kreuger (1880–1932) and Clarence Hatry (1888–1965) were once-successful businessmen whose businesses eventually ended in bankruptcy and disaster, largely because of fraudulent practices. Alexandre Stavisky (1886–1934) was an infamous embezzler. — Ed.

state of tension that we open our daily papers with a chill of apprehension lest Armageddon may have already begun. Nor do I mean merely that greed and covetousness constitute the greatest of the influences making for war. I mean that chicanery, fraud, and robbery are undermining that sense of confidence in one another that men must possess if they are to work with any heart or enthusiasm, trade with any hope of gain, or amass riches with any prospect of enjoying them.

A modern novelist, in a work written as early as 1915, describes a banker and some friends at a circus, watching a dangerous performance on swinging trapezes by a troupe of acrobats. The scene suggests a parallel. After writing, "Bankers have spun fine threads covering every land with a web of credit, infinitely complex and so delicate that a child's hand could tear it," he makes the banker talk thus to his friends:

> If bankers in any country doubt the solvency of those in any other, if there's the slightest hesitation, an instant's pause of distrust or fear, a very ugly smash ensues.... Nobody knows we're doing it. Nobody sees our flights through the air or guesses the supreme confidence we bankers must have in each other. Someday, something will go wrong. A rope will break, or a man will miss his grip, and then people in one place will be starving while people somewhere else have food all around them rotting in heaps. Men will want all sorts of things and will not be able to get them, though there will be plenty of them in the world. Men will think that the laws of nature have stopped working—that God has gone mad. Hardly anyone will understand what has happened—just that one trapeze rope has broken or that one man has lost his nerve and missed his grip.

When we slip a trick, it will be on the audience we shall
fall. It will be the people who will be bruised and crushed
and won't know in the least what has happened.

How prophetic these words were in 1915 we all saw in 1929,
when high finance slipped many tricks and fell upon the whole of
humanity, causing unemployment on the vastest scale ever known.
And if a mere loss of nerve or lack of skill could shake the system,
roguery and double-dealing can be twice as destructive of that fi-
nancial confidence that is necessary for world credit. Yet what have
nations and individuals been doing since 1918 but repudiating
debts public and private in an unprecedented way? Why wonder,
then, that trade is not recovering or prosperity returning? How
can prosperity ever return until a general spirit of honesty among
nations and individuals comes to prevail? Yet far from coming to
prevail, it seems to be vanishing more and more.

Nay, we are often assured that what is really wanted is the
abolition of this virtue altogether. For that is what is involved in
the doctrine of communism and of class war, in the perpetual
incitation of the "have-nots" to seize and confiscate the posses-
sions of the "haves," in the widespread insinuation that all who
now possess possess unjustly, and that those who do not possess
have been robbed by them. The title-deeds of property hitherto
acknowledged are called in question. The very acquisition of it is
stigmatized as unsocial.

On the lips of somewhat saner and soberer critics, capitalism
at least is roundly condemned, and its complete overthrow is held
to be the first step in the reform of society. This puts the Church
in a peculiarly painful dilemma. The present capitalistic system
really arose over the ruins of the only social order the Catholic
Church had any responsibility for. In so far as capitalism has a

religious background at all, that background is Calvinism. And in its later developments, capitalism has progressively concentrated the possession of wealth in the hands of a relatively small number, who thus dispose of the lives of the majority in a way that almost necessarily leads to exploitation and that has had most deplorable results. Left to itself and its own inhuman code of ethics, it becomes the very Mammon of the Gospels against which Our Lord warns His disciples (see Matt. 6:24). Enthusiasts, therefore, say, "Let us get rid of it altogether." But the question arises: Can we in the present circumstances of society take such a drastic step without producing chaos and even greater misery than at present? That its power must be curbed and its abuses remedied is clear enough. But we must have a workable alternative capable of carrying on our highly developed civilization with its countless millions of workers. That must never be lost sight of.

It is the fate of these countless millions that alone engages my sympathy. I do not want to see a collapse that will condemn them to die like flies in winter.

The only alternative hitherto translated into practical politics is the so-called communism of Russia. But, first, this is no longer communism except in name. Indeed, its very founder, Lenin, had to abandon many features of the system the moment he faced reality; and his followers have gone on slowly metamorphosing it into something only distinguished in name from the slave-system of the ancient world. By what must be the master-stroke of irony in all human history, the most grandiose attempt ever made to get rid of capitalism has simply substituted for a loose corporation of capitalists, whom their victims could play off a little one against the other, a narrow oligarchy of capitalists, highly and efficiently organized to stifle every criticism of their despotism, who, having seized effective control of all the sources of wealth in a vast region of illimitable possibilities, give the individual citizen a sort of Hobson's choice of carrying out their will or else of dying by hunger, by the firing-squad, or by overwork and cruel treatment in prison camps.

And they could hardly avoid it. For if we really think down to fundamentals, we shall see that either we must abandon civilization altogether and revert to a nomadic state or else overcome the laziness inherent in human nature by compulsion or bribery or some form of enticement capable of keeping ordinary human nature at tasks that must at times be tedious or distasteful. The ancient world chose compulsion—that is, the dominant castes forced all the rest to work or die under the flagellum. This inhuman policy has been slowly mitigated into the policy of wage-enticement—an unsatisfactory one, it is true, but at least an improvement on the crude brutality of the slave-gang. Capitalism is the ultimate evolution of this process. And no one can be blind to its many defects or shut his eyes to the increasing friction with which it functions.

Yet enthusiastic reformers must really let themselves remember that it has also many most remarkable achievements to its credit. Every single great invention that has revolutionized life—the steamship, the engine, the train, the telegraph, radio, cinematograph, airplane, printing press, newspaper, motor car, bicycle—owe, if not their discovery, at least their exploitation and extension to capitalism. Further, capitalism has conditioned the enormous increase in the populations of the world that the last century and a half has witnessed.

If, then, we are to scrap it, what is to carry on the production of the multiplied complex machines that have become a necessity of life? What is to afford employment to the two billion people inhabiting the earth? The state, say the state-worshippers. But how? The state must overcome the laziness of the individual by some incentive or other. Of course, if the state could alter human nature and make everyone so devoted to the new god as the saints were to the old, there might be some hope. And many ardent zealots really seem to think that somehow this will come about. Yet what prospect is there of a race of men who will all rival St. Francis of Assisi in a disdain of the riches of this world? And is it not the nth power of the insane to found such a fantastic ideal upon the preliminary denial to man of all hopes of a future life?

The partial success of the Soviet experiment is here utterly deceptive. To begin with, it had to beg, borrow, or steal a whole host of things from the capitalistic nations. Secondly, it had to exercise the most thorough-going tyranny on the vast majority of its subjects. For a wage, which gave, on the whole, a far higher standard of comfort than Russian workers have known and left the earners some little liberty, the Soviet leaders instituted a system of bread-tickets and a police force that has never yet been equaled in ruthlessness or terror-inspiring efficiency. They set up a "ticket-of-leave" society over a fifth of the world.

Even so, they have been compelled gradually to recur to wages, and now they are harping on the absurdity of equal reward for unequal service. So they are scaling wages, according privileges, and admitting the right to trade and barter. In a word, after churning up the life of a whole continent to its very depths, they are gradually subsiding into a social order that will reproduce in time the worst features of the old capitalism and add a whole crop of its own. Meantime, in international relations, they are back to that game of diplomacy that they repudiated and anathematized as one of the worst evils of capitalism. They are showing in the game far more finesse and less scruple than ever did the ministers of the tsar. A new Russian imperialism is emerging before our eyes, and, while it professes pacifism, it is militarily more formidable than ever were the Romanovs; while it professes communism, it is gradually creating a new oligarchy of slavedrivers more hypocritical than were the Roman patricians, who had at least the frankness to call a slave a slave.

I am afraid, therefore, that pending the arrival on earth of a completely new race of men, we are perforce compelled to take stock of human nature as it is and to accept its limitations, its inequalities, its cupidities, and its possession of free-will, with the inevitable consequence of much abuse of this great but perilous prerogative. The most we can do is to canalize a little the direction of man's free energies, control a little by moral education his dangerous passions, and evoke as far as may be his nobler instincts. Justice, charity, pity, self-abnegation, a sense of brotherhood, an ambition to contribute something to the common stock of ideas, to the universal wellbeing—these surely would help to lift a little the cloud now resting on the minds of men. They will never usher in the millennium. But this most dangerous mirage is really responsible for half the mad schemes we hear hawked about by dreamers of vain dreams, which go to the head like fresh poteen and create the nightmare world we are forced to live in.

Over against these wild conceptions, all of them consciously or unconsciously based upon the denial of the individual soul in men, all of them uniquely concerned with his body and his brief existence here, all of them divorced from any reasonable explanation of the purpose of that existence, the Church sets a quite different ideal. She says: "You have not here a lasting city but seek one that is to come" (see Heb. 13:14).

"Dope," say our polite friends in Moscow, "to enable the bourgeoisie to rob the proletariat." But the same evangel who tells us we seek a city to come also tells us with equal emphasis that we shall never enter it if we rob anyone on the way thither (see 1

Cor. 6:10). Hence, there is something wrong somewhere, some very grave misunderstanding. Our adversaries might at least show enough critical perspicacity to see that a philosophy that points to a reward really worthwhile for service done here—the service precisely lying in the love of and labor for our fellow men—has at least a certain intrinsic potentiality for brightening life. A teaching does not become "dope" because it is scornfully rejected by many and half-heartedly embraced by more. It may be true and only await wider acceptation to show its intrinsic worth.

There never was a better social maxim uttered than the strange paradox, "Seek ye therefore first the kingdom of God, and His justice, and all these things shall be added unto you" (Matt. 6:33). If any single generation of men really lived up to this maxim, a good number of our agonizing social problems would disappear. But when our manifold sins involve us all in a common and universal disaster, many of us blaspheme against God. This is sheer idiocy, of course, and it gets us nowhere. For if there were a God, blaspheming against Him is a more ludicrous proceeding than a dog baying at the moon; if there were no God, why, even then blasphemy would resemble multiplying naught by a hundred naughts, which gives you nothing as a result, however long you continue the absurd process. The world crisis will not be remedied by blasphemers railing at "this sorry scheme of things" and seeking to "shatter it to bits" in the vain dream of remolding it "nearer to the heart's desire." It calls rather for that "sober sense and awe of things divine" that Euripides extols.

But many raise an objection here. They say why do men like you condemn communism when you yourselves practice communism? And the answer is because we know what it means, what it presupposes, what its consequences would be if, instead of being a counsel of perfection observed by an insignificant proportion of mankind, it were made the basis of human society. We defend men's right to possess private property for the same reason that we defend men's right to marry, though we have taken a vow that puts marriage out of our power to contract.

Occasionally in history crack-brained ascetics have condemned marriage altogether—the Encratites and Manicheans of old, the Albigenses in the Middle Ages. But the Church, which had to fight against sensualism to uphold the vow of celibacy, had to fight still more against the fanaticism that assailed matrimony. And it is significant to observe that every such movement of fanaticism led inevitably not to greater purity but to such promiscuity that both Church and state had to combine to suppress the disorders. The Church has had no harder task than the simple humdrum obligation of keeping its head when fits of cerebral disturbance were sweeping over the world like tidal waves and threatening to destroy society. The Church opposes communism, not because she does not love the poor, but just because she does love them; not because she is insensible to the bitterness of their lot but because she is acutely sensible of it; and has had to fight, often to martyrdom, in order to prevent that bitterness from growing to intolerable dimensions. The Church is hostile to no noble ideals. She is only suspicious of crazy ones, knowing from long experience that they necessarily increase the very evils they pretend to cure.

If I dwell on this big issue so long, it is because I feel that a great deal of the dishonesty practiced today springs from the wild gospels being preached to the suffering masses of mankind. These are being indoctrinated with the view that if they are poor it is because somebody else has robbed them; and that it is their right, even their duty, to compensate themselves at the expense of anybody and everybody who now has anything. The victimization complex grows and spreads until stealing, cheating, pillaging become invested with a certain halo of revolutionary romance; they are shots fired in the great battle for social justice and the redistribution of the world's wealth. It does not occur to anyone that the wealth of the world may vanish altogether in the violent process, and that at the end there may be a hundred poor people where there was one before.

The Church looks before and after; the demagogue knows nothing of what has gone before and cares little for what may come after. Enough for him if he can make a noise today, raise a barricade, burn a temple, shoot a monk or nun—both notorious capitalists, though neither owns anything personally! So the wild phantasmagoria moves on until a few shrewd, ruthless ruffians seize the prevailing chaos as an opportunity for grasping the scepter, shooting on the wrangling mobs, and setting up their rule in a world gasping with exhaustion, bleeding at every pore, and fundamentally poorer than when the witches' cauldron started to simmer over.

Meantime the dwindling and disheartened remnant of sane, sober, industrious folk have got to plough and sow and reap and rebuild the ruins that were once their homes—not castles, perhaps, or palaces, but some shelter at least against the wind and rain. They only know that children cry for bread, and need clothes, and look up to them with wistful eyes. And so they somehow struggle on, staggering under a burden that ages them, breaks them, and makes them long for death. Happy for them if even in death they can see the stars of Heaven shining above a world where God has not gone mad, as blasphemers mutter, but man has.

Unlike your soap-box preachers, I have no panacea for the ills of humanity. I have no five years' plan, or ten years' plan, for making you all happy, prosperous, contented. I cannot, like Karl Marx, give you in a phrase or two the complete clue to the interpretation of history. Still less can I present you with a magic formula that will rescue you from your manifold distresses. I can only say that I think the fear of God and the love of God a necessary prerequisite for any happiness whatsoever, here or hereafter; the practice of justice all round and toward all an indispensable condition for the working of any social or political system you may dream of erecting; the exercise of charity, a coping stone to the edifice of Christian sociology. I know all this looks poor and pallid by the side of the glowing promises of your apocalyptic prophets, who germinate in a perishing society with tragic fatality and dire consequences. But I know of nothing higher, holier, or more conducive even to temporal prosperity than the Gospel of Christ; and I do think that we might really give this venerable message a real trial before rejecting it for hot gospels that have no relation to reality, and leave the facts of history and the nature of man out of account. Remember that whenever and wherever men have taken it seriously and striven to live up to it they have found this sin-and-sorrow-laden world bloom suddenly with strange flowers wafted from celestial climes—the followers of the Poverello, for example, who saved Europe in the thirteenth century.

> They muse on joy that will not cease,
> Pure spaces clothed in living beams,
> Pure lilies of eternal peace,
> Whose odors haunt their dreams.

If this be "dope," I wish we had a little more of it. It tastes like nectar; and, unlike the raw alcohol of the New Evangelists, it does not lead to madness. It causes neither blood-pressure nor "Katzenjammer," as our German friends style the headache that punishes drunken excess. It is not stored in the cellars of Champagne or the vaults of Bordeaux. But it is a real drink, a Lethean cup, whereof who drinks straightway forgets both sorrow and pain. The saints have drunk deeply of it; and they have told us of its inebriating quality. If our palates are so coarsened by the "hooch" of this boot-legging world that we fail to appreciate it, ours is the loss; and that loss is felt even here and now.

Mankind is almost literally afflicted with *delirium tremens* from the heady and medicated beverages served up to it in its taverns. What it really needs is the wine of Cana. Only it will not hear of miracles, remembers Jesus, if at all, as a rather pathetic Jew of long ago, who, falling foul of the ruling authorities in His time, was put to death; and retains the name of God chiefly for swearing purposes. At the same time it raises a cry of alarm over the danger to "our Christian civilization"!

It is important to remember that justice and honesty bind all manner of men—the rich as well as the poor, the rich perhaps still more than the poor. Dishonesty on the part of a rich man is clearly more utterly criminal and inexcusable than on the part of a poor man, who can plead a very moving human excuse for his sin. It is usually on a far vaster scale and inflicts far greater damage on a much wider circle. The dishonest financier gambling with the savings of numerous clients, who seek to put a little by against old age, is so base a miscreant that hardly any punishment seems too severe for him. That is obvious.

Yet what I would like to stress, for it is easily forgotten, is that every act of roguery or dishonesty is really at the expense of the poor. I wish I could make this clear. The immediate victim may be a rich man, but the ultimate victim is the community, and that consists of just you and me and our several worthy neighbors, who have all an almost forlorn battle with adversity all their lives long.

For surely it is evident that only honest industry creates wealth. Only the steady worker at some useful job—which may, of course, be very varied in character—is contributing anything to the upkeep of the community. The mere idler is a parasite, a detestable fungus growth, who ought to find the food he eats choking him when he remembers that he has done nothing to earn it. But the rogue is not merely a parasite—he is a public enemy. He is increasing the odds against the honest man in such a myriad of subtle ways that the ordinary unthinking person has no notion of them. Let me illustrate by a few concrete examples. Employment depends upon successful industry. This in turn depends on honest treatment of the worker, honest work by him, honest trade, honest transport. The man who does not work honestly is doing his little best to bring the factory to ruin and thus *disemploy himself and his comrades.* The carter, or carrier, or transport official who is dishonest is running up prices unduly, and thus robbing the consumer and lessening the market for the product. The profiteering trader is acting similarly. And all are conspiring to increase the cost of living, which hits everybody, but first of all and most cruelly the very poor, who hover always about the starvation line. Surely this is clear.

Similarly the people in business premises, large or small, who practice even petty peculation are heading the whole concern for bankruptcy, which involves every one dependent on it—the owners, shareholders, managers, and employees. But there is more: the feeling of distrust chills enterprise and prevents men from launching out into new ventures that might lessen unemployment. I have known men who said they saw the possibility of starting new businesses or enlarging old ones, but did not do so because they felt that, when they had sunk their money in the concern, they could not rely upon a square deal. They would be faced by difficulties of every kind, making life a nightmare and the end the workhouse.

If you speak to merchants about high prices they reply: "But we must budget for a large and growing percentage of bad debts. Many who could pay won't pay. So we must increase prices to cover losses. Besides, overhead expenses are mounting up on all sides; taxes, rates, transport, everything is soaring. Hence, we must increase our demands upon the purchasers." Yet, once more, we have the vicious circle. Higher prices for them lessen the market and ultimately make even the high prices unavailing. We know that governments, the most skillful of all predatory bodies, soon learn that there comes a time when to increase the percentage of taxation is only to lessen the yield. Saturation point, so to speak, has been reached. And saturation point in high prices can be easily reached.

We shall never get anywhere, we shall never see social peace or economic development, unless we realize that the interests of all are as interwoven as a seamless robe. I do verily believe that this theory of class-war is not only a highly immoral doctrine, but literally the most stupid and suicidal doctrine ever formulated. The exploiting capitalist is an immediate enemy of labor, but almost a worse enemy of capital, and should be put under the ban. He is Public Enemy No. 1. But the lazy, inefficient, or dishonest employee or worker is, again, immediately an enemy of capital, yet more so, perhaps, though indirectly, of labor, for he is doing his best to rob these and their children of the very bread of life. He is Public Enemy No. 2.

Labor and capital are like man and wife. They must somehow make up their quarrels and adjust their differences, or both come down in ruin. Nor can they then call upon the state to find indefinite funds to bridge over their respective claims. For, after all, what is the state, economically considered, but labor and capital? And the state cannot by any necromancy give to any product a value above its worth in the present economic order. A camel cannot live indefinitely upon its hump—the hump dwindles, and the animal dies; yet today whole nations are pursuing a policy of living on their hump—that is, of tiding over recurrent crises by calling upon reserves. These are dwindling. It is the exact policy of a man who, inheriting an income of £10,000 per year, proceeds to live at the rate of £15,000 per year. It may be fine while it lasts, but how long will it last?

No, my dear brethren, sanity no less than religion, makes it clear that even for temporal prosperity a community needs honesty, justice, moderation on the part of all. It needs peaceful cooperation among all its units. I care not who a man is, or what his place in the economic plan, he must do his job as well, as honestly, as faithfully as he can, or he is positively working for the general impoverishment. A rogue may, indeed, occasionally get away with it. If he does, then no doubt he is so far forth the richer for his crime. But first of all, he loses his own self-respect, and cannot be really happy. Secondly, he is an enemy of the community, including, therefore, his own class. Enlightened public opinion should judge with unsparing sternness the thief, the cheat, the profiteer, the exploiter, the saboteur, the malingerer, the brutal egoistic man of greed wherever found. He is really a vulture preying upon his fellowmen in general. He is the foe of all honest toilers in every grade of life.

He is, finally, at enmity with God, who has said: "Thou shalt not steal ... Thou shalt not covet thy neighbor's goods." To him are addressed those words of St. Paul: "You do wrong and defraud: and that to your brethren. Know you not that the unjust shall not inherit the kingdom of God ... nor thieves, nor covetous ... nor extortioners shall inherit the kingdom of God" (1 Cor. 6:8–10).

6

Honesty and Charity in Speech

Thou shalt not bear false witness against thy neighbor.

—Exodus 20:16

As justice is the basis of business relations between men, so truthfulness is the basis of social intercourse, which rests on the confidence each one feels in the words of his neighbor. Lying is anti-social. Even where lies apparently work little or no immediate harm, they have a tendency to sap our trust in human veracity and make us suspicious of everything we hear. Their effect is like that of petty thefts, which, if multiplied, send a sort of creeping paralysis through the whole world of commerce. And both may be compared with those septic foci that physicians search for in glands, or gums, or tonsils, or joints, when a once vigorous constitution shows signs of collapse, knowing that those foci are perpetually ejecting into the bloodstream infinitesimal doses of poison that, in their cumulative effect, can be ultimately fatal. Hence, falsehood has everywhere and always been under the ban of society. It has incurred the stigma of being a peculiarly mean vice and has been punished by the contempt of men rather than by their indignation.

The epithet of liar shares with the epithet of cad the unenviable distinction of suggesting vileness unredeemed by manliness or any quality we could admire.

"Hateful to me as the gates of hell is the man who has one thing on his lips and another in his heart." So sang Homer in the dawn of all our culture, incidentally giving, in perfect form, the technical definition of a lie. And hateful he remains even today, when many older maxims of morality have been questioned or denied. Religion endorses this vehement reprobation, adding a higher sanction: "Lying lips are an abomination to the Lord," says the book of Proverbs (12:22); and in Sirach we read, "Falsehood is a vile reproach in man."[24] No one, therefore, has a good word for it.

Yet it flourishes and spreads, like those prolific and ineradicable weeds that invade the husbandman's fields, defy his industry, and half neutralize his toil. Further, it works far more havoc than the unthinking dream. It distorts men's views even on the most important issues of life. It generates bad blood between the nearest relations. It causes many of those tragic misunderstandings that lie at the root of family discords, tribal disputes, and even national antagonisms. In wartime, it is used as cold-bloodedly as poison gas. Indeed, a distinguished soldier has frankly avowed that when he got young lads to train for the slaughter-yards in Flanders, he had first to fill their minds with faked atrocities and false propaganda against the enemy. Otherwise, he said, how could you make decent, kindly, and humane youths ready to plunge exultingly a gleaming bayonet through the vitals of other equally decent and kindly youths who are separated from them by a few yards of No Man's Land? He drew, to his credit, the wholesome

---

[24] Author's translation of Sirach 20:26. —Ed.

lesson that this, too, made war an unmitigated curse that all should conspire to ban.

He might have added that if lying were first sufficiently banned, war itself would disappear. For lying, widespread, deep, inveterate, must have gone to poisoning the relations between peoples before passion rises to the detonating point. Men in the mass are never just gratuitously wicked or gratuitously foolish. They are molded to wickedness and folly alike by a minority who are wicked and thrive upon human credulity.

> Were half the power that fills the world with terror,
> Were half the wealth bestowed on camps and courts,
> Given to redeem the human mind from error,
> There were no need of arsenals and forts.

Think of it! We might have disarmament all round if half the military estimates of the nations were spent on correcting error, of which the chief creative agent is falsehood. A world press, for example, entirely bent on telling the truth, the whole truth, and nothing but the truth, might make the League of Nations unnecessary. And if at Geneva all the various representatives were speaking truth and seeking truth, instead of trying to bluff and bluster, outmaneuver and outlie their rivals, that institution would very likely function.

In the tragic history of the Church's fight for existence and for the right to preach the message of Jesus, what a part sheer mendacity has played! How its teaching has been travestied and its conduct aspersed! The Divine Founder Himself was condemned on perjured testimony. His apostles inherited the struggle with the powers and principalities of darkness obscuring truth. The early Church, which really held out to Rome the only hope it had of regeneration and survival, was persecuted through three whole centuries because it was supposed to be sapping the foundations of the Empire. And moderns like Gibbon have not shrunk from endorsing this perverse view.

In the sixteenth century, the unity of Christendom, and with it the principle of European solidarity, was destroyed by men who have poisoned the very wells of history, until even today the most conscientious student is bewildered and at a loss to know the truth that, though often far from edifying and instead often saddening in its manifestation of human weakness or downright depravity in high places, is quite compatible with all the claims of the Church, when these claims are dispassionately examined and rightly understood.

Now the lies have done their work and are more or less abandoned, and they are replaced by others better adapted to the new environment. But always, the father of lies is busy disseminating misunderstanding of all things Catholic.

For example, the idea still prevails, as a sort of precipitate from earlier calumnies, that the Church's doctrine on truth itself is weak, shifty, and demoralizing. No prejudice is more widespread than that against casuists, who, particularly when they are also Jesuits, are supposed to have raised lying to the dignity of a science or an art.

Casuistry is as necessary and as honorable as jurisprudence. It is as old as Cicero, who in his *De Officiis* and other philosophical works has quite fine examples of it. Further, Catholic casuistry is a strict science; it is based on fundamental principles, firmly held and logically applied. It must at times be subtle, for the very simple reason that the problems of human conduct are indefinitely complex. The Quaker, for example, says with Scripture: "Let your speech be yea, yea: no, no" (Matt. 5:37), and he thinks he has given a complete rule for all human utterance. To all such, the test query may be put: "Have you ceased beating your wife yet?" (If he is not married, substitute mother or sister.) What shall he answer, Yea or Nay? Your simple Bible Christian will generally be found in his counting house to be quite as shrewd a man at guarding his personal or business secrets as the "wiliest" of Jesuits, and he will fall into casuistry without knowing it. Most likely, also, it will be indefensible casuistry at that.

The Catholic—including Jesuit—teaching on truth is not less strict than that of non-Catholic moralists. It is stricter. It states categorically that all lying is sinful, whereas other systems say it is sinful—except when it is not. In other words, there is really no system at all; there is no basic principle whatsoever. We cannot be content with that. Neither, on the other hand, can we forget the fact that men often have secrets that they are free to guard and sometimes bound to guard, even at the expense of their lives. What, then, is to be done?

Obviously, if a mere refusal to speak suffices to guard the secret, no more is permitted. But often, this is not enough. When it is not enough and the secret must be preserved, you may lie as you please, say non-Catholic moralists. No, say Catholics, but you may use mental reservation—that is, you may put the Paul Prys[25] off the scent by answers that admit of a double interpretation and so are evasive. Remark, first of all, that this is not lawful unless you have a right to your reticence and the inquirer has no claim to know the truth. If he has a claim to know the truth, he must get it, even if the truth is unpleasant for the speaker or involves serious consequences for himself or somebody else. Thus, in courts of law, men are often under the most stringent obligation to give truthful testimony, though they know it will mean the loss of their

---

[25] Title character of John Poole's 1825 play who was known for being incessantly inquisitive. —Ed.

suit. The idea, which seems to prevail so widely, that witnesses can simply fence and lie as they like is, of course, utterly immoral. It tends to make the administration of the law impossible. It defeats the interests of justice in a hundred fatal ways. It puts a premium on chicanery and fraud. It enables criminals to escape the penalty of their crimes and thus encourages them and others in the commission of more crimes. Carried far enough, it can paralyze the operation of law, in which case, the ordinary, well-meaning citizen is handed over to the tender mercies of the rogue or the bully.

Mental reservation, therefore, is for Catholic theology the *via media* between lying and the betrayal of secrets that we are entitled or bound to safeguard. An example will illustrate its use. Let us suppose a suspicious husband comes to a confessor and says, "Father, my wife went to confession to you recently, and I want to know whether she admitted that she was putting arsenic in my food." It is clear, is it not, that the confessor must not break the seal of confession, even if it meant the loss of his life. Suppose, now, he realizes he is dealing with a madman and feels that simply to reject his impertinence with scorn will infuriate him perhaps to murder, he can say, "My dear friend, you are completely deceived. I never saw your wife in my life" — meaning that out of the confessional, he never met her, and in it, he did not look at his penitent at all. This statement is sufficiently true to avoid the reproach of being a lie, and it is adequate for preventing one of the worst sins a priest could commit.

It is open to anyone to say that this is subtle doctrine liable to abuse. That may be quite true. But not all subtle doctrine is false; and there is hardly anything in life that is not capable of being abused. The alternative teaching that you may in difficulties say whatever you like, first of all, abandons the fundamental principle dominating the whole question; and secondly, it is only far more liable to abuse than the permission of mental reservation, which is not a "Jesuitical" invention to encourage falsehood but the sincere effort of the Church to meet a difficulty of the acutest kind that can arise. Our critics are always in the happy position of having no intelligent or coherent system of theology, philosophy, or ethics to defend, none of the hard human problems to resolve that confront the priest from hour to hour. It suffices them to pick up any cobblestone or lump of mud from the street and shy it at the great Gothic temple of "Romanist" theology. They feel no sense of obligation to erect some alternative shrine where men can worship in security and peace.

As to the reproach that this teaching tends to make men in general shifty, evasive, or insincere, it is answered by an appeal to facts. Look up the state trials of England since the Reformation. See where Catholics stood in the dock to answer with their lives on accusations perjured to the core. Contrast Thomas More, Bishop Fisher, Cuthbert Mayne, Edmund Campion, Robert Southwell, and Oliver Plunket with the whole cohort of their adversaries, from Thomas Cromwell, Henry VIII, Elizabeth Tudor—the most fluent and shameless liar in an age of falsehood—Robert Cecil, Shaftesbury, Titus Oates; and judge for yourselves who loved truth and who practiced lying.

Or read again the controversy in which Charles Kingsley, author of "Westward Ho!"—a travesty of history—argued that Cardinal Newman by reason of his conversion had lost his Anglican birthright of unswerving truthfulness; and then, again, ask yourselves on which side stood sincerity and passionate dedication to truth. For my part, I would trust the great cardinal's lightest assertion more than many a man's Bible oath. The simple fact is that lying, evasion, insincerity, and even perjury can be found in any large body of human beings, whatsoever code of ethics they pretend to follow, and, contrariwise, men may have a delicate sense of honor and veracity without knowing very explicitly the philosophy of the issue.

One thing, however, is certain: Catholic teaching gives as little encouragement to lying as to murder, theft, or adultery. It says categorically, "Thou shalt not bear false witness." It does not, indeed, ask its children to let hostility or malice inveigle them into the betrayal of their own or other people's legitimate secrets. Here, as always, it deals with life, the hard actual reality, which does not lend itself to embodiment in a few neat phrases or sonorous maxims. It sees its adversaries desert their maxims the moment they are placed in a dilemma. It knows that Pharisaism and fine professions are little guarantee of moral conduct. It has been for many centuries the victim of a thousand lies and, what is worse, half-truths, distortion of its teaching, aspersion of all its works and ways. But it neither falters nor wavers. It just goes on, and for the most part lets misrepresentation die of inanition, knowing that truth has all time for its vindication and that if, like justice, it is halt of foot, in the ancient phrase, it is also great and will prevail.

All lying is hateful, abominable alike in the eyes of God and man. But when lying not merely offends against truth but against justice, obviously it has a two-fold malice. And that it does frequently so offend needs no proof. We may briefly consider some of the instances.

1. Calumny is defamation plus falsehood.

Defamation itself is often sinful even when true. If I know a secret of another, the revelation of which will hurt his feelings, lessen the esteem in which he is held, injure his prospects, or cause enmity between him and his friends, I am not justified in proclaiming it merely because it is true. No doubt, there are times and circumstances when I may or must do so. Others may, for one reason or another, have a strict right to the knowledge, which outweighs his claim to my secrecy. I may be called as a witness in court; I may feel that only by revealing the secret can I prevent some great evil either to an individual or the community. Many such contingencies can be imagined that unseal my lips to speak out even at the expense of the party in question. The only obligation is to remain strictly within the bounds of truth and certain knowledge. We must not exaggerate nor give rumor or conjecture for anything more than they are worth, which is very little.

2. But calumny is always sinful and doubly sinful. It may, of course, be light and rather frivolous than serious; it may thus escape the guilt of mortal sin. But it is never lawful. In its more serious form, it is a peculiarly odious thing and is often associated with very sinister designs. In public life, it is at times exploited to make men, or policies, or institutions odious preparatory to some fierce assault upon them. The origin of it is often hard to trace and would, of course, be found rooted in utter malice. But once it is started down the whispering galleries of gossip, it is taken up by many who are prejudiced, no doubt, but yet not wholly insincere. For all that, they can hardly escape responsibility. We are told that for every idle word that man shall speak, he shall render an account at the Day of Judgment. Well, here is a word that is more than idle: it is wicked, and someday, the reckoning will have to be paid.

You all feel how cruel a wrong may be inflicted by calumny in ordinary social intercourse. A charge of dishonesty may ruin a man's business prospects; a suggestion of malpractice in the case of a professional man may mar his whole career; a lying innuendo against a girl's virtue may destroy her chances of matrimony; against the fidelity of a wife or husband it may wreck a home.

Such statements will generally owe their origin to jealousy or some mean, secret hatred that corrodes the speaker's heart. Or it may spring from rivalry and conflicting interests; it may be part of the plan of an eager arriviste to supplant one whose post he covets, whose higher reputation stands between him and the place in the public eye that he has convinced himself belongs by right to him.

Ambition is a passion, and, like all passions, it has its legitimate place in life. Saints may forego it, and do, and act well in doing so. But it has its place in the teleology of things. It stimulates energy, promotes industry, and inspires the ordinary man, for whom pure love of God or humanity is too high a motive to constitute an effective appeal. Hence, it makes for the progress of the world. This is the reason why society in its own interests offers the highest rewards it has in honor and emolument to those whose achievements seem to merit them. We encourage youth to excel by conferring prizes for excellence in sport or study. There are purists who condemn this as bad pedagogics. But such purists either live too remote from life and expect from average human nature more than it can give, or they are confusing, as so often happens, what is of counsel with what is of precept.

The world advances through men passionately dedicated to high ideals of attainment, and the motivation behind such ideals may be very varied. It may be of the very noblest, and this certainly is most likely to carry a man to the summit of attainment. It is the motivation of saints, great artists, great scientists, great craftsmen. Yet he will be exigent indeed who will condemn the artist, the scientist, or craftsman for seeking recognition, or even a little more material remuneration for his arduous toil. If only he seeks this by genuine achievement, who can reasonably complain? "Poeta laudatur et alget," wrote Juvenal long ago—"The poet is praised indeed, but shivers in his attic." It has often happened since then, and we feel that it is poor enough justice when afterwards men raise statues in the poet's honor or mourn his premature death from pneumonia. Let us not be too hard on anyone manfully and honorably seeking his due place in the sun.

On the other hand, ambition can be a most dangerous and even devastating passion. It can "wade through slaughter to a throne and shut the gates of mercy on mankind." In the case of lesser men, it can be the parent of all sorts of low maneuvers, dishonesty, or falsehood. It can eat out all the manlier traits and decencies of the heart. Such a man will not stay to ask whether what he says of rivals is true or not. If he shrinks from grosser calumny, as likely to recoil on his own head, he will at least verify the well-known words of Pope:

> Willing to wound, and yet afraid to strike,
> Just hint a fault, and hesitate dislike.

The subtlety of the innuendo, however, hardly lessens the malice of the calumny. Rather, it increases it.

3. Gossip, the bane of social intercourse, deserves a word to itself. Often it is mere garrulity, one of the various pathetic expedients by which men and women seek to escape from the hideous emptiness of their own internal lives. They have no higher interests, no hobbies, studies, or pursuits capable of chasing ennui. So they gather in little knots and discuss their neighbors by the hour, one reason being that, through lack of culture, they are incapable of discussing anything else. There is no interchange of ideas—at most, there is the parrot-like repetition of whatever ideas are floating around in their social milieu, which, in their egoism, they are apt to identify with the world of thought. There is mostly only a tiresome comparison of personal judgments about mutual friends.

To call all of it wrong, sinful, or uncharitable would be an exaggeration. But much of it consists just of those "idle words" the gossip may one day be called upon to answer for. And much of it may be worse. It may be that subtle mixture of defamation and calumny that we call bitter gossip and that is little less than a social plague. Oh! not a major crime, not amenable—at least, not always to juridical condemnation; but a detestable thing that corrodes social intercourse, causes alienation among lifelong friends, and works all sorts of ugly mischief in life.

Sometimes, it springs from the desire to be witty. Now, this desire is not criminal, though it is often very vain. But the true humorist is mellow and kindly and tolerant. If he laughs at humanity, that humanity includes himself. The modern literature of humor, in some of its representatives at least, seems based upon the idea that in laughing at human foibles, you must trample human nature into the mud. Cynicism, sourness, and gross indecency are its chief ingredients.

There are even authors whose whole intellectual outfit seems to consist of scorn of mankind expressed in the vocabulary of the house of ill-fame. Their own evil humors ferment and boil over into pictures of life where not a single character retains a vestige of human decency. And they call it realism! Perhaps they are somewhat justified. It may be a real reflection of their own souls. But as a picture of the world we know, the variegated earth of Plato, it suggests a charcoal artist who has no other color than black. When such writers—who, in Thackeray's mordant phrase, see life bloodshot—pretend that they are out to reform mankind by insulting it, they just add hypocrisy to calumny. The ordinary sinner knows full well that he has enough to beat his breast about, but he is conscious also of one or two surviving loyalties or redeeming qualities in his soul. Hence, the criticism of these somber satirists leaves his withers unwrung. He might be amenable to the raillery of an Addison or a Goldsmith; he can feel only a hardening of the heart, a stiffening of his obstinacy under the brutal blows of a Swift, or the almost sadistic, inhuman cruelty of an Anatole France.

Ordinary gossip, of course, has neither the merits nor the defects of such master calumniators. It cannot flagellate mankind. It can only distill an alchemy of quiet malice into suggesting that Miss X is ten years older than she admits; that Mrs. Y keeps strange hours or dubious company; that Mr. Z has a very rubicund complexion and a redder nose. It can "hint and chuckle and grin" and leave it at that. It is just a nasty meanness that ought to have only one consequence—a boycott of the gossiper.

4. When falsehood is affirmed on oath, we have perjury. There is little need to add that this duplicates the sin, which becomes a violation of the second as well as the eighth commandment. Little need also to remind anyone that it is deplorably frequent in the lawcourts of the whole wide world. In our own country, judges and lawyers have again and again commented on the unblushing effrontery with which men and women will enter the witness box, call God to witness that they will tell the truth, the whole truth, and nothing but the truth, and then proceed to defeat the efforts of the ablest lawyers to extract any truth at all. So great has been the abuse in certain places that perjury has been made a reserved sin. Yet it is difficult to awaken the public conscience to the enormity of it.

Let us see if we can do anything to make its malice a little clearer. First, it is a lie; secondly, it is blasphemy; thirdly, it is a sin against legal justice; fourthly, it is nearly invariably a sin against commutative justice. The first two points are evident. The third is often overlooked. Legal justice demands of us respect for the laws of the land in which we live. I assume here that these are themselves just and passed by legitimate authority. Even where the authority in question is not legitimate but usurped, such laws as have for their end the promotion of the public weal—as distinct from the strengthening of a usurpation—are binding in conscience, because the common good demands this. And, at any rate, I am envisaging perjury in the normal functioning of equitable law. In this case, a man sins against his duty as a citizen. He is, as far as he can, impeding the administration of the law upon which depend the peace and progress of the state. He is unpatriotic, whatever he may think himself. He is promoting anarchy and crime, because he is rendering the punishment of crime impossible. He is creating an impunity for the rogue, the cheat, the highwayman, or the murderer. And we have before our eyes in Ireland, North and South, glaring proof of how impunity can foster crime. This is, indeed, the one valid argument for the death sentence. There are man-destroying tigers in human form, who seem only amenable to the fear of death. If this sanction becomes inoperative, such men will seize on any pretext, even the pretext of religion, to perpetrate atrocities that would be incredible if they were not too manifestly real.

Yet they can often procure perjured alibis, escape the scaffold, roam the world in freedom, and plot the murder of still more victims of their bloodlust. If this goes on long enough, civilized government breaks down, and all the citizens hold their lives under the precarious tenure of criminals' caprice. Terrorism spreads and pervades the whole atmosphere. The very sanction that should guard life is turned against society to put the life of every man at the mercy of gangsterdom. It is happening under our eyes in many lands, even, I fear, in our own. And the reprobation of the majority of decent citizens does not affect the assassins at all. They know they can rely upon the lurking sympathies or play upon the fears of a certain section of the population to defeat the law. Knowing this, and being utterly devoid of conscience, they seem to glory in making each succeeding murder more spectacularly monstrous than those that have gone before. They themselves are beyond the reach of any appeal. But what about their abettors, who either know their guilt and help to cover it up or, still worse, are ready, perhaps, to go up into a witness box and swear a false alibi? They make themselves participators in the campaign of crime. They risk becoming, in legal terminology, accessories after the fact. The most charitable excuse that can be pleaded for them is moral or physical cowardice.

Perjury sins against commutative justice when it is committed, as so frequently occurs, to cover up or facilitate fraud or wrong done to the neighbor. How multifarious such perjury may be, how frequently it is exemplified, needs no elaboration. In countries where divorce is legalized, it is notorious and avowed that perjury reigns supreme in suits for divorce. We, fortunately, escape this fertile source of perjury. But in litigation about land, debt, or family feuds, with what unblushing effrontery sworn witnesses will lie! One would imagine they had never heard the divine commands: "Thou shalt not bear false witness"; "Thou shalt not take the name of the Lord thy God in vain" (Exod. 20:16, 7). They take it wholly in vain. It seems to add no measure of added veracity to their words, and they appear to regard perjury as a fencer might regard riposte or tierce. Well, they may win their cases in the courts of man. But they shall one day stand before a Judge who needs no witnesses, who will have full cognizance of all they ever said or did, and woe betide the perjurer in that hour! Human justice may be baffled or defeated. Divine justice is mysteriously patient but ultimately triumphant; and its judgments, when they fall, are final, irrevocable, inerrant, and eternal. To doubt this is really equivalent to doubting God.

If anyone be inclined to think I am exaggerating the influence of falsehood, I beg him to reflect a little on life and the forces shaping it. Public opinion is to human life almost what gravity is to the world—a vast, mysterious, invisible pressure determining ultimately the destiny of mankind. It has been compared to snow. What lighter or more negligible than a snowflake? What more formidable than vast masses of snow? In the glacial age, whole tracts of the globe were covered with snow and ice, and their physical configuration was modified forever. We see still on our hillsides and mountains the striation produced on the hardest rocks by snow!

The strongest tyrants and despots fear public opinion even while defying it. Their *oderint dum metuant*[26] is the merest bluff. They are forced to use their very despotism to mold opinion in their favor. Hence, almost before the arsenals and magazines of a country, they seize upon the press, the radio, the cinema, the theater, the music hall, and particularly the schools. They must dispose public opinion in their favor or they know that ultimately their thrones will topple like a city shaken by an earthquake. If the mass-mind is properly enlightened, if men in general are allowed to know the truth, if fair argument and honorable appeal to reason are alone practiced, if facts are first established and debate conducted with the sole purpose of elucidating them and handling them wisely, then there is hope of sound policy prevailing. At least false-hearted, diabolical wickedness will be avoided, for masses of men are not wicked, they are only wax in the hands of wickedness.

But when angry and excited disputants, eager for the triumph of their own views at any cost, distort facts, invent lies, and hurl insults, Wisdom veils her face and flies. The plain people looking on are either bewildered or infected with the passionate absurdities

[26] "Let them hate provided they fear."

of one side or the other. Public opinion is poisoned, and men rush at one another's throats. Trotsky wrote of a certain Russian orator: "He did not appeal to the head or the heart, but to the blood in men's veins." That type of oratory is one of the world's major plagues today. It shouts at us with epileptic frenzy from the hustings in slogans, shibboleths, catch cries, war cries; it glares at us from posters disfiguring our walls, hoardings, public places; it revels in half-truths and noisy falsettos; it seeks to hypnotize by sheer audacity of assertion and profession, as certain advertisements simply hypnotize the ladies by promises of more fat or less fat, more hair or less hair, more color or less color—at 7 shillings, 6 pence per box! Why, they will offer to bring back our dead friends in astral bodies—at 2 shillings, 6 pence per séance! Our age might be called the age of ballyhoo.

And the object is by any and every means to mold public opinion, which is the Archimedes lever for moving the world. Today, that lever looks as if it would lift the world from its hinges. At least, it is threatening to hurl reason from its throne and produce pandemonium throughout the globe. Yet the human mind was made for truth and can only rest in the consciousness of possessing it. The lie is thus at fundamental variance with our nature. It poisons the wellsprings of our happiness. It works always and everywhere in the interests of its father, the devil, who was a liar "from the beginning, and he stood not in truth; because truth is not in him" as St. John tells us (8:44). Its triumph is everywhere and always a triumph for antichrist.

About the Author

Patrick J. Gannon was born in Cavan, Ireland, in 1879. He entered the Society of Jesus in 1897 and was ordained in 1913. He was a professor of theology at Milltown Park for thirty-five years. Known for his eloquence, Fr. Gannon was frequently called upon to preach, and he delivered lectures in Dublin and in other places in Ireland. Some of these lectures were collected and published as books. Fr. Gannon also wrote several pamphlets and numerous articles. He died in 1953.

Sophia Institute

Sophia Institute is a nonprofit institution that seeks to nurture the spiritual, moral, and cultural life of souls and to spread the gospel of Christ in conformity with the authentic teachings of the Roman Catholic Church.

Sophia Institute Press fulfills this mission by offering translations, reprints, and new publications that afford readers a rich source of the enduring wisdom of mankind.

Sophia Institute also operates the popular online resource CatholicExchange.com. *Catholic Exchange* provides world news from a Catholic perspective as well as daily devotionals and articles that will help readers to grow in holiness and live a life consistent with the teachings of the Church.

In 2013, Sophia Institute launched Sophia Institute for Teachers to renew and rebuild Catholic culture through service to Catholic education. With the goal of nurturing the spiritual, moral, and cultural life of souls, and an abiding respect for the role and work of teachers, we strive to provide materials and programs that are at once enlightening to the mind and ennobling to the heart; faithful and complete, as well as useful and practical.

Sophia Institute gratefully recognizes the Solidarity Association for preserving and encouraging the growth of our apostolate over the course of many years. Without their generous and timely support, this book would not be in your hands.

www.SophiaInstitute.com
www.CatholicExchange.com
www.SophiaInstituteforTeachers.org

Sophia Institute Press is a registered trademark of Sophia Institute.
Sophia Institute is a tax-exempt institution as defined by the
Internal Revenue Code, Section 501(c)(3). Tax ID 22-2548708.